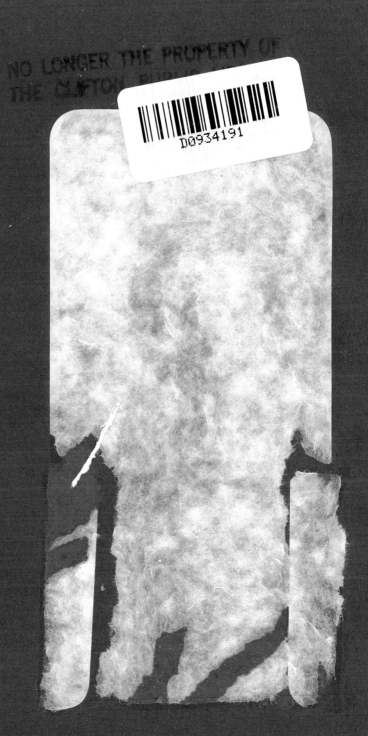

Wild Goose, Brother Goose

Books by Mel Ellis

ADULT
Wild Goose, Brother Goose
Softly Roars the Lion
Run, Rainey, Run

JUVENILE
Ironhead
Sad Song of the Coyote

Wild Goose,

Brother Goose

➤ ➤ ➤ ➤ ➤

➤ ➤ ➤ ➤ ➤

by MEL ELLIS

HOLT, RINEHART AND WINSTON
NEW YORK • CHICAGO • SAN FRANCISCO

FIRST EDITION

Library of Congress Catalog Card Number: 77–80332
SBN: 03–081845–1

For Gwen
With respect, admiration and love

FOREWORD

*D*UKE AND DUCHESS, the geese in this story, once lived at a place called Little Lakes which is the home of the writer. The goose, Duchess, was pinioned so could not fly, but the gander was not and had the option of staying or following the flocks down the sky. Many times he was tempted, and many times he left, but he always came back.

Then a dog killed the goose, and when the gander became disconsolate, he and his four goslings were taken to the Horicon Marsh National Wildlife Refuge and turned free among tens of thousands of Canada geese. He made the trip to the refuge in a burlap bag, so he never saw by what route he had come.

He stayed away that winter, but in spring he was back home and with another goose. How the gander found his way back is one of the mysteries of the wild society.

Why he didn't stay, but only visited for a week, is no mystery. Calling to him across thousands of miles and thousands of years were the great Canadian grass flats where lazy northern rivers spread into wide sloughs.

This time there was no problem. His goose could fly. So one morning they haronked good-bye and lifted to join a passing flock.

Geese live long, so perhaps even as you read this, Duke is somewhere. The remainder of the book is fiction.

7

Tonight I heard the wild goose cry
Wingin' north in the lonely sky . . .
Wild goose, brother goose, which is best,
A wandrin' foot or a heart at rest?
                    —"Cry of the Wild Goose"

Wild Goose, Brother Goose

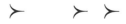

>-

*H*E CAME OUT OF a tumultuous
sky into a captive flock of his own kind, and while waiting out
the storm among the manmade ponds which floated earthbound geese, took one of them as his mate. When the skies
cleared and his wild flock lifted, he went with them, and
when she did not follow, he came back clamoring for her to
lift, ride the wind, come with him to a far northern delta to
build her nest.

She ran along the dike, wings flailing, but the right one
had been pinioned and the long feathers furnishing the ulti-
mate thrust were lost in the operation.

Until dark, and even after, he winged low over her, back
and forth, clamoring. Then, when it was obvious she wasn't
going to follow, he put out his webs, braked with his wings
and surfed along the water to settle alongside where she sat.

They spent the night together, but the next morning he
rose again to the clamoring of a passing flock, and insisting
that she follow, went down the sky until even she, with an
eye for scanning horizons and an ear for hearing worms walk,
could no longer see or hear him.

She waddled out of the water and sat disconsolate on the
bank, her neck tucked in and her feathers so ruffled a man
knowing geese might have suspected she was ill. He had

taken her and they were mated, and now he had gone, and this was not in the code of the wild things which unite goose couples for life and sometimes, for one or the other, beyond the days of living.

So when another gander of the captive flock came importantly over, she ignored his compliments, and when he put out his long neck to offer her a bill of bright coontail moss, she thrust out at him and he gathered in his pride and went back among the flock, seeing if there was yet one he might want and who would want him.

There were many geese on the clustering ponds, which was, among other things, a trout ranch where people paid to come and fish. The geese were local color, all dealt flightless soon after birth, so they could only swim across the ponds and graze the dikes so people might have at least an illusion of being in some north country where trout caught rising flies instead of pellets of meat and cereal flashed from hoppers by electrically timed devices. For generations these geese had been earthbound. Sometimes still they clamored when the skies from dawn to dusk were etched with passing flocks, but the days of longing to be airborne became only minutes of mourning with each passing generation as the will to freedom was lost in the fine fat of feeding.

The mated goose kept an eye on the sky and an ear turned to the north. Like a maid met, married and carried across the threshold, she could not believe it was only for the night, but that soon now, at any minute, he would reappear and come to claim her forever.

All day people came to catch trout, and all day goose couples kept breaking away from the flock to go off and establish their territories where barrels had been put down for them in an orchard, among a grove of birch, where oaks grew. . . .

But the mated goose did not rejoin the flock, because she no longer wanted to be sorted out and walked off. Instead she sat alone on the water, and the spoons and spinners and the flies of the fishermen fell close, and sometimes when a trout was hooked, the water from the flailing fish would fly over her, and the people remarked about how lonely she looked out there, and why didn't she move with the flock or go off with another goose to where the barrels were.

But she kept an eye on the sky, because it is not in the ways of Canada geese to take love lightly. If there was to be any frivolity at the Silver Sun Trout Ranch, let it be among the mallard ducks which flirted shamelessly, accumulating wives and stealing hens one from the other with much fighting and raucous quacking.

The Canada geese were monogamous. They courted with quiet dignity, and unlike the flighty ducks, the gander remained with the goose, protecting her on the nest and protecting the goslings even after they were flight-borne and until they went off to form alliances of their own.

So the goose kept her eye on the sky, and when darkness came she stood on one leg and put her bill around into the feathery nest of her wing, but always her whole being was tuned to his tones, which, though only briefly heard, would be instantly recognized so long as she lived.

So she passed the night, and the goose flock resting on the water and the couples back on the higher ground around the barrels were mostly silent, and only the uncivilized ducks quarreled, even in the dark. Fish splashed as one or another trout sampled hatching insects and found them less substantial than the meaty, vitamin-filled pellets with which they were fed.

Morning came abruptly when storm clouds which had been gathering reversed direction and dropped back off the edge of the earth to plague some other place and the sun became a suddenness of bright light.

The goose put down her leg and tilted an inch to come square. First she stretched one leg and wing hard backward, and then the other. Then she ruffled her feathers, shook vigorously and walked to water. She stepped off the bank, and giving a few powerful paddles, coasted along the pond's surface a little way and then dipped her bill to skim and lift a morning drink.

She ruffled her feathers again, and bowing gracefully, dipped her head into the water so a silver stream ran down her long neck and over her gray back. Bath finished, she shook and the pond was broken into gleaming ripples and the spray from her feathers showered like diamonds.

The flock was loud now with impatience, and even the pairs walked away from the barrels toward the hard-packed circle where the corn was spread. It was time, and the geese knew it as surely as they knew at what moment the automatic feeders would erupt pellets for the trout, so they might crowd around and steal from the fish.

So they came, ducks and geese, to the hard-packed arena because it was time Tom Rank came with the corn.

Then, right on the chiming of the hatchery clock which

regulated work hours for Tom and the men, for machinery, water flow, food distribution, for the many other automatic and man-manipulated devices, Tom stepped from a long, green warehouse where the food was stored.

He liked feeding the geese and ducks. He liked watching the trout scramble for pellets. Though a foreman at the ranch for nearly twenty years, he had never gotten over the excitement of feeding time. He liked to hear the geese honk and the ducks clamor, and to see the trout splash, and watch the excitement of it run like electricity through the flock and infect even the song birds, so the cardinals whistled piercingly above the bugling of the geese back where the fence supported grape and bittersweet, nightshade and wild cucumber in clinging vines.

John Mackenna watched too, though he took no part. He came out of the kitchen door and stood under the shadow of the porch, and if there was a nostalgic undercurrent in the mainstream of his thinking, this was understandable, because the flock was his and he'd watched it grow from a single wild pair, and in the beginning, and for many years, the job of feeding had been his.

Mack came often through the kitchen from his office, which had been attached to the house like an afterthought, to stand briefly and watch the men at their chores. There was no spying in this, no looking to see if every man was working, but a need to leave his paperwork and mentally return to that place at which he'd started.

Tom Rank carried two large yellow plastic pails from which corn spilled as he walked. His eyes swept across the converging flock to the stragglers coming in from the barrels and then out over the water of the six ponds to where the single goose sat alone.

He whistled brightly, thinking the lone goose might come to his feeding signal, but when the bird turned and swam slowly the other way, he scattered corn, and then whistling again, hurried to check in the men who were arriving for work.

Mackenna saw the lone goose too, and another time he might have slid a skiff into the pond and herded her to a dike and gently coaxed the bird behind wire, to see if, by chance, she had been injured or was sick. But now he turned away.

The flock gobbled the corn so quickly, a few couples did not get to the arena in time, so now these moved to where the ponies were pastured and began grazing. The main flock went for a drink, and then drifted off the water to eat grass, and some mated couples were off to the barrels to see about nest-building, and a few birds, not yet mated, began bobbing and weaving, the courtship dance which aroused the other geese, even the yearling nonbreeders, into emulating the couples with matrimony in mind.

But the deserted one stayed aloof almost as if, mated but hardly married, she had been ostracized from polite flock society.

Gradually the flock filled with the new green grass snipped from under fencing where ponies could not reach, drifted back to water, and those not yet ready to set up house-keeping bunched together in a feathery flotilla and half-asleep and half-awake let the breeze drift them to a shore from which they paddled lazily to open water to drift again.

It wasn't summer, but it felt like it, and the hatchery help was waiting for the yellow fish eggs spread on trays to hatch and for the helpless fry to fall through the screening and lie waiting for strength from their yolk sacs. Under a warm sun the incessantly chattering sparrows were carrying breast feathers of the geese to eaves, and the crows, usually so noisy, came and went with a shadowy black stealth because there were eggs in a nest in the fence-line oak. Red epaulets of blackbirds flashed as boundary quarrels erupted into aerial combat, cock robins screamed hysterically at one another among the apple trees, and lecherous mallard drakes raided their brother's harem and were in turn cuckolded when their backs were turned.

But the geese entered placidly and contentedly into the creative partnership with nature, and except for the lonesome goose, there was at least no outward evidence of discontent.

Twice young ganders detached themselves from the flock which seemed held in a cottony content, and swimming an invitation to the lone goose, acted as though they hadn't made an offer when they were rebuffed and returned with an indifferent stroke to slyly see if some other had finally made up her mind.

Only once did the lone goose cry out. It was when a hawk came sailing, and there so high in the sky no man might see, she caught the wing beat in her eye and for a second thought *he* had returned. But the clarion of hope guttered in her throat, and she bent her head to look down at the water where even the reflection mirrored her dejection.

So the noon hour came, and for spring the sun was so hot

on the shore, violets all opened at once and apple buds prematurely plump showed pink through coats of thin scale.

And in the unseasonal warmth, birds and even the mallards quieted and the siesta had a fine accompaniment of soothing insect sounds as winter survivors and newly hatched insects swarmed up out of the ground and water and from dead wood and from under the bark and up from the straw and leaves and out of cracks where the dry cold of winter had spread boards, until the air hummed and even water-born dragonflies just dried in the sun flashed jeweled wings.

It was during this quiet time that the call came—clear though distant, high and carrying as a silver horn. The lonesome goose gathered her feathers tight, lifted her head and swam and then tried to lift in a frantic and futile beating of water.

Some of the other geese in the flock heard it too, and they answered, and Mack, hearing the geese, came out from his office to watch, and then the lone goose stopped trying to fly and cried out with a creature's longing for creation.

Then there was a speck on a far horizon, growing larger, until the goose saw the glint in the gander's eye and heard the powerful beat of his wings and saw his neck bend as he put his head down to look upon her. He did not come directly down. Once he knew she was waiting, there were other considerations.

He was a *wild* goose. He was wary. He would never so much as land near the trees lest they be hiding a predator, and so the sheds and the shining wire and the trucks and men walking and the white house all meant incredible danger.

Instead he called to her to come, follow him, that he knew of a wild place where only the moose came, and sometimes the wolves . . . but man rarely, if ever. He pleaded with her to know her duty to him now that they were mated and leave the water and climb so they could fly beyond where the land was a checkerboard of fields fouled by the sprawl of cities with stinking breaths.

He insisted that she lift and fly north a thousand miles to a river where there were spits of gravel to come to and broad flats of grass now that the spring floods had run off into the channel again.

And she tried, until her wings were dragging like the wings of a wounded goose which has been chased a long way. She tried until the pond was glistening with bubbles and the frightened trout had gone to the bottom. She tried until her bill came open and her breath was hot in her lungs.

And then when she could not get even a few inches off the water, she put out her neck and lay flat, and she could not even answer when he called, and he circled closer and closer and lower and lower and the men stood among the buildings watching and Mack stood leaning against the porch rail wondering. Then, with the sun at his back, he put out his webs, braked hard with his wings and planed along the water to come alongside her.

He stayed close but did not touch her. The men went back to their work, and Mack went back into his office, and a few of the captive flock came a little closer to see better. Then she lifted her head and he bowed a few times, after which she drank some water and, typical of mated ones, he took water too. Then they swam to the far shore, and she would have led him to the grazing grounds, but he would not leave the water.

She went up the shore and started toward the trees, but when he refused to follow, she went back to him, and they made hardly audible noises as they swam together like a royal couple on parade—back and forth so the captive flock could see them well and take notice that they were a pair so there would be no misunderstanding among the young bachelors, especially since it was obvious there were too many ganders for the geese on hand.

Then once again she swam to the far shore and started toward the orchard, but he could not find it in him to risk going among the trees where every kind of danger might conceal itself.

Members of a flock long captive might walk among such crowded places, but one as wildly wary as this one must have long, flat fields where a fox could not hide and even a mink might find it hard to get close without being seen. Delta country, that was his kind of land. Flat and reaching. Or wheat fields cut to stubble and stretching to Manitoba or Saskatchewan horizons, or big water flat to the farness of seeing.

But little cramped corners with trees were more frightening to this gander than the storms which sometimes pulled his flock out of the sky. He could not abide them, like a wolf cannot abide farmlands, nor a moose high mountains, nor a wild goat broad valleys. He must be able to see. He must be able to stand head high and know about every moving thing within range of his eyes.

So when he would not follow, she swam again with him to the exact center of the pond, where he felt safest, and there they stayed and there they were when Mack came from his office and called over to Rank. The foreman hurried over.

"Maybe you'd better try to get that goose into a pen, or that gander will take her down the creek and to the river. Then next fall if she doesn't get shot, she'll freeze in the ice when winter comes and there'll be no way to help her."

"I know," Rank said, and he went to the pond, and the wild gander swam nervously to the far shore, his head high, wanting to fly but waiting for the goose to loft first.

"You're a wild one," Tom said. He often talked to the geese, as Mack once had, and neither saw anything strange in it.

He walked around the pond, and the gander led the goose back to open water and across to the opposite side. So he went to where the tiny skiff was overturned on the bank and slid it into the water, and kneeling in it, stroked with a short paddle, so the goose and the gander were forced against a shore.

The gander stood it until the bow of the skiff was turned at him and coming straight. Then he ran a few steps on the water, and clamoring loudly, beat down the air with his wide wings and lifted into the sky.

The goose tried to follow, but only managed to skid along the surface with a wild wasting of energy, and then when Rank expertly slid the boat parallel, the bird was forced to land. Quickly he beached the skiff, and then spreading his arms, began to herd the goose slowly toward a wire enclosure with a door wide and waiting.

Overhead the gander climbed a hundred yards and began circling, calling down for the goose to come, that the man would kill her if she didn't, and how now didn't she know it was time to be moving north to where the grass was still new and tender and the flats were still soggy from the spring floods.

And the goose called back that she couldn't fly, but the gander could not understand how it was she could not fly. Couldn't all geese fly?

At the door the goose would have eluded the foreman, but he was expecting it, and rushed her through the door and quickly swung it shut. Mack, still on the porch, turned and went inside.

Then the goose walked up and down the wire, lifting and lowering her head to find some way out of the enclosure. Up and down, while the gander circled and called, and Rank went for corn, and the captive flock, nervous now, began to add to the clamor of the wild one above them.

Twice while Tom was scattering corn for the goose, the gander flew so far he was only a speck in the sky, but each time he returned, and then when Rank went to put the pail away, the gander dropped down into the far pond and swam anxiously in every direction as though not believing his mate was not where he had left her.

The door to the house opened and Mack came down the steps. Rank came over, and he asked: "Do you think he'll stay?"

"It would be better if he went."

"Perhaps," Rank said, "but what do you think? Will he go, or will he stay for the summer?"

"I think he will stay," Mackenna said.

"Perhaps we'd better leave her out then?" Rank made it a question.

"You know what would happen. They'd go to the river. A flightless bird doesn't have a chance. If she lives through fall, the winter will get her. Which would you prefer?"

"I don't know what you mean," Rank said.

"Do you prefer the goose has a little heartbreak now and lives, or goes with him and dies? Which do you think is better?"

Rank looked thoughtfully out to where the gander was swimming. Then he said: "I don't know. I honestly don't know."

"Well, think about it," Mackenna said, and Rank didn't have to be told that Mack was prescribing a little longing in the beginning rather than heartbreak in the end.

Still he couldn't quite agree, and looking up at the taller man he said only: "Maybe."

Mack had had his own heartbreak, and it had made him brittle. But Rank did not plead the goose's case, ask that she be let out, because Mack was boss, and sometimes since his wife had died he did not take as kindly to suggestions as when she had been living.

Marcia had been dead nearly five years, but she'd lived long enough to see the trout ranch grow from a dream into reality. Along with Mack she'd stood to see the muddy waters seep up out of the earth to fill the great craters the huge draglines had dug. She'd seen the silt settle and the sun shine straight down through ten feet of water to where you could see a silver dime on the blue, marlaceous bottom. She'd seen the cedars rise and the spruce groves put up higher and higher spires. She'd seen the pair of ponies come, and she had seen their young born, so there'd be mounts for their customers' children. She'd seen the first pair of geese grow into a flock, and that it was a slave flock never occurred to her. She'd seen the maples they'd lifted out of a neighbor's woods come mature enough to redden in fall.

Tom Rank had been there to watch it too. He had been Mack's first full-time employee. Then the days had been feverish with activity. Together the pair had planned, and then like boys they'd go to the house for Marcia's approval.

Evenings Rank would go home to his own family in a house he bought on an abandoned farm a few miles from the ranch, and Mack and Marcia would sit on the porch where they could look out over the spread and consider if they'd forgotten any ways to better soil conditions, improve water resources, overcome the limitations of men and machines.

It had been a gigantic do-it-yourself project involving great earthen dams, huge concrete spillways, conifer windbreaks, daffodils, tulips, iris, ducks, fish, stone banks and sod banks, orange tiger and less flamboyant day lilies, special corners for wildflowers, grape arbors, kennels, a swimming place, and a long cool stone hatchery where millions of eggs could turn into millions of trout.

Marcia had lived to see the mortgage burned, to see the diminutive Tom Rank be made foreman over a score of helpers and to see on her husband's face the glow of satisfaction from a dream realized.

Then the telephone call, and Mack could always remember the doctor's exact words: "It's cancer and I'm not going to try to fool you, John. It looks ominous."

That was five years ago, and in the interim women had slid in and out of Mackenna's life, and though Tom Rank hoped that one might come to live in the house where Mack rattled around alone, none had.

That is why Rank felt Mackenna's bitterness was a larger part of the decision to keep the geese apart. Perhaps, Rank reasoned, Mack did not want to be reminded about the urgency of love.

So Rank turned and went from the porch to the hatchery, and he heard the screen door bang as Mack went back into the house. The banging door, like a gun shot, went all the way across the ponds to the last one, where the gander floated, and he turned his head sharply from left to right, looking for danger, but he did not go—not that day.

THE SUN LOWERED and in sinking lost some of its warmth, and when it touched the horizon there were cool eddies of air coming on little currents up from the creek, and east from the big spring hole where cool water ran through many pipes and troughs and vats to give oxygen and life to eggs and little trout.

The sun sank without much of a fire, slipping away like a white disk over the edge of the earth, and the gander lifted when it was down and flew over the pen in search of the goose, which had been making muted, plaintive sounds. He swooped low, saw her behind wire, and then beat his wings more swiftly to rise.

He went up and away on a long slant and then turned and came back again. He was so high there was bright daylight all around him, and he could see the shining edge of the sun. But below, the ponds, sheds, houses, woodlots and the pen where the goose waited were becoming shrouded as night lifted higher and higher, until it came to the highest place he could go.

It wasn't until fullest dark, and after circling without a sound, that he angled down. Then, just above the pen, while still a hundred yards up, he spilled air from his wings and slipped like a skimming stone from side to side and down and down, to brake at the last moment and come to the packed earth inside the wire.

She came over to him then, and in the dark they stood together.

$\succ$ $\succ$

*I*N THE MORNING, after their night together, no one saw the gander leave at dawn, nor did the goose call for him to stay, and instead of pacing back and forth to probe the wire, she crouched down on her webs and watched him lift. When he was a few hundred feet high, he slanted down toward the far pond, and there is where Rank saw him when he came from the green shed with the corn.

So, after feeding the flock and throwing some on the ground for the goose behind the wire, he went to the far pond and scattered a little along the shore and in the shallow water, hoping the gander would come over to eat.

But the gander had gone over to the far shore, and when Rank walked away he did not go near the corn, fearing it might be a trap. Instead he picked at what grass he could reach without going ashore, and nipped tendrils of plants growing in the water. He was too wary to submerge his head, to tip up and find more succulent fare. He even found little stones for his gizzard from the shoreline at the water's edge, and then when the help began to arrive, he ran on the water, and lifting into the air, flew the quarter-mile to where the Rose River moved placidly in its shallow valley.

He sat on the water for a long time just drifting with the

29

lazy current, and then, satisfied that he was alone, edged toward shore and starting feeding.

There was a south wind, but with such an edge of crispness that it made yesterday's promise of a quick, hot summer seem immature. More geese were in the sky, again riding the wind, and sometimes he called out to them, because a goose alone is like a man lost.

But though they called back and sometimes lowered their flocks to see what was so enticing as to tempt a lone goose to stay behind, they never stopped. Once he winged from the water and intercepted a V of more than a hundred birds, and tucking himself onto the tail end of the formation, flew until the ponds were so far behind they looked like drops of water on a green leaf. Then, with a little cry, he dropped out of the pocket in the air stream and turned back.

Some of the geese, especially those few who had not found ganders, called out an invitation to string along and find a summer of fulfillment in the land of little trees.

But they did not bay with the persistence of flocks southbound in fall. Spring flocks rarely did. They flew with more purpose, wasting only enough time in any watering place to eat and rest long enough to fly farther.

Fall flocks, more than half of them youngsters, bayed like beagles at every green field, every other resting flock, every marshy bay, and even down to the duck gangs. Sometimes in fall, young snow geese and specklebellies of the year, having lost their parents to guns in the provinces, joined the great Canadas. It was a laughing thing for people to see the smaller birds wing frantically to stay with the formations of the big birds and to hear their excited yelps in contrast to the clarion bugling of the Canadas.

But now in spring the snows and blues and white-fronted geese had consolidated their flocks, and so far as the Canadas were concerned, there was no time for checking out stubble or corn fields, grass flats or spreading bays, because each had a date with such destiny as he'd been hatched for, and the time was upon them, and if they wasted it, that time would be gone, and forever.

So, when the big gander dropped back, the flock did not waver as it might have in fall. Instead it drove north and west a little, relentlessly counted progress on the big rivers and lakes which swept to the south beneath them.

The gander dropped lower and lower, and then turning, came to the Rose River, and flying at treetop level, went all the way back to where he'd been sitting when the flock went by. He ate again, and on feeling full, came to where an old muskrat house was a soggy decay of last year's moss, climbed on it, and lifting a leg, leaned a little to rest.

There were no predators. Only ducks flew back and forth, and the water floated coots and gallinules. Sandpipers ran the shore, and little rails toured the pads of lilies only days out of the water and still so freshly green it was hard to believe some-day they would be dark and leathery enough to hold a bull-frog on top and hoard enough insects along the underside to feed a sunfish.

When the sun was directly overhead, the gander put down his leg, and ruffling his feathers, shook vigorously so each fell into its precise place and he was smooth as a velvet goose.

Then he walked down off the heap of rotting moss and frightened a muskrat which had been critically eyeing the structure as if to decide whether it was worth repairing or whether it should start a new house in some other place.

In diving, the muskrat splashed loudly, and the gander gave an involuntary cry of warning. Then he slid out into the current and sipped water. Ruffling and shaking flat again, he turned into the wind, and flailing with his webs, was airborne.

He flew to the trout ranch and came silently over the pen where the goose stood. He uttered no sound, and neither did she, and it was as though they had come to some understanding and there was no need for further discussing it.

Having checked to see that she was safe, he glided to the far pond and came down on the water. The corn was still there. He had seen it glinting yellow along the bank and under the water. Now he swam slowly toward it, and when within a dozen feet, stood off to look over every bankside blade of grass for some signs of a trap. Finally he edged over, and picking up a kernel, toyed with it between his bill and then dropped it. He picked up another and felt it with his tongue before swallowing it. Then the gander ate six kernels swiftly and swam back to the comparative safety of the center of the pond.

When Tom Rank checked that evening he was still there, and after he had whistled in the captive geese for feeding, he came down to the pond and talked, because the sound of the human voice, if persistently and calmly employed, can sometimes dispel the fear in wild things.

"So, you're going to stay," Tom said. "So why don't you

go join the Duchess. No one is going to hurt you. She is a duchess, you know. A duchess in her ivory tower. Have you mated with Duchess? I think so. In that case I'll call you Duke."

And so the gander got a name—Duke. And it fitted, because he was a beautifully arrogant bird. His throat scarf of white reaching all the way around on either side almost to the top of his black head was like a royal choker, a badge of distinction. It marked him brightly as of the elite. He was big for a second-year gander, perhaps ten pounds. He stood well over three feet and could stretch his black neck until his head came to a height of four. His bib was white. It washed away to gray beneath, and along to a flaring white rump patch, and his back feathers were like metal, gun metal—like the hard, smooth steel of chain mail.

While Rank talked, Duke swam nervously, turning his head from left to right so that no matter which way he was positioned on the water he always had the man in his eye.

"I won't bother you," Rank said. "But I see you didn't eat much of your corn, so I'll not bring more. Now just take it easy, easy, easy, easy. . . ." And the gander stopped swimming to speculatively eye the softspoken man.

Finally Rank went back to his chores, and Duke swam back to the middle of the pond to wait for the sun to set. As soon as it was dark, he lifted and silently flew over to the pen and dropped down beside the Duchess. She came over and he put out his long neck and touched her across the back, and she settled softly until she was flat to the ground waiting for him.

So the pattern was established, and the Duke lived out

each day along the river or eating sparingly of the corn in the far pond, but at night he came to the Duchess. And it must have been enough for them, because she never probed the wire again to see if there was a way of escaping that she had overlooked, and he did not call out anymore to the passing flocks, nor did he lift to follow them.

They had been living together perhaps two weeks when Mack came from the house one warm night to walk through the orchard and smell the apple blossoms and see how white they were in the light of the stars.

He was amazed at how the night could soften all the rough edges and harsh realities of day and make even the fencing look lacy. Then he went down the gravel path which led past the wire which held the Duchess, and when nearing the fencing he was startled, and stopped in surprise when a large shadow lifted with a ripping of air to loft above the building and fly smoothly and quickly west toward the river.

Then Mack, who rarely laughed these days, did so, but it was softly to himself. So that is how it was that in the night the wild gander came to his lover. He stopped by the wire, and looking over the top to where the Duchess stood watching him, said: "Well, make the most of it old girl, because when the snow gets deep he'll go."

The goose bobbed her head as though to assent, but of course she was only doing what geese sometimes do when people talk to them.

He stood for a while watching the goose and wondered if Tom knew, and supposed that he did, because it was hard to hide anything from his foreman.

He stood a little while longer, and then hearing the swish

of the gander's wings above, turned and went back to the house.

Next morning was Saturday, and with high school boys to augment the regular help, Rank turned the Duchess free to graze so she could get such greening things as are necessary for a Canada's health. He herded the goose beyond the pony pasture to where a long, narrow field was lush with short grass, and then he sat on a stone fence under a billowing white cloud of plum blossoms.

The Duchess made no move to graze, but wandered on down the field with her head held high. Then she called out and ran a little way. She stopped, and turning her head from left to right to scan all the sky, she called again.

Down on the river Duke heard the call and lifted into the air. He flew to the trout ranch and passed over her at a height of a hundred feet. Satisfied now, Duchess began grazing while Duke flew patrol back and forth.

Under the plum tree Rank remained quiet, so finally Duke glided down and landed at the far end of the narrow field. Duchess started running, but then slowed to a walk, and stretching her neck low, weaved slightly as she walked. Duke accepted her invitation, and coming close, presented her with grass.

Then after a while they grazed together, and finally when Rank got up and came to the end of the field, Duke flew back to the river and Duchess went willingly to her place behind wire.

Satisfied that they were mated, Rank went to the orchard, and selecting a barrel which no couple had claimed, he carried it to the enclosure which held the Duchess and set it firmly in a corner against the small shed. Then he went on up to the house.

Duchess went at once to examine the barrel. She pecked at the nail heads along the bottom, tried the iron rim around the top with her bill. A dozen times she went away from it and then came back to inspect it again. Then she picked up a small twig, and extending her neck, placed it in the barrel. After that she ignored it.

When Duke came that night he inspected every crack and every nail and every nail hole in the old barrel. Duchess did not join him during the inspection. Finally he bobbed as though in approval and came over to pay his court to the goose.

So they lived, together nights, and on Saturdays Rank took Duchess to the green field and they walked together in daylight. Gradually a nest took shape in the barrel, but the geese in the orchard already had goslings before Duchess presented Duke with a large white egg. He inspected it much as he had the barrel before accepting it as theirs.

Then immediately he became a sentinel. No longer did he dally to court her at length, but took her swiftly and then stood guard, his long neck always extended and his wedge-shaped head turning from left to right with bright eyes investigating the toad's hop, an owl's patrol, a bat's swift winging, a nighthawk's ruffling mutter of wings—every sound and movement down to the drop of dew splatting from an eave to the round barrel top.

So it was that after the fifth egg had been laid, and during the pre-dawn dark which is blacker than all the rest of the night, the little wind which had been blowing went away and such a silence came as lifts men from their beds even as quickly as a loud noise, and even brings all wild things awake.

In the white house, dimly huge like a mother hen among a clustering of lesser buildings, John Mackenna came awake, and he went to the window to see if there was any light yet in the east, and he wondered about the geese. But it was so dark he went back to his bed but for a while he could not sleep because of the stillness.

In the kennel the five dogs uncurled and lifted their ears. In the pasture the five ponies, each sleeping on three legs, stood four square and stretched their necks. Mallard ducks chucked softly, and the pigeons ruffled on their roosts, and in the pens where there were pheasants the cocks stretched their necks, and Duchess put down a leg to tilt an inch and come straightly erect.

But it was only an interlude of wakefulness, and in a little while all these creatures except Duke came into harmony with the weather change, and ruffling, curling and leaning or twisting, closed their eyes and went back to sleep.

But Duke tilted his head until a bright eye was focused on the darkest place where the shed overhang cut out even the light of the dimming stars. There was something there, something in the blacker band of shadow, something silent as fur.

The gander lowered his head and stretched his neck as though the better to see and hear. He was so delicately tuned to the earth's turning that he could hear the uncurling corn which grew in several rows a little way beyond the wire. He not only had a sixth sense of acute perception of things neither seen nor heard, but a seventh sense which instantly and accurately diagnosed even another's intent.

Though the gander could not immediately identify the danger, he knew something was there. Then it moved, putting one paw down after the other as lightly and as softly as the touch of milkweed silk. Yet Duke heard. He braced himself and waited. Then when the feathery sound of sleep was again in all places around, the mink moved swiftly out of the shadow.

Whether it actually intended to attack or was merely passing was of no importance to Duke. It was heading in the direction of the eggs and where Duchess stood. So he coiled his neck like a snake ready to thrust, and when the mink was in range the flint-hard bill darted direct as a flight arrow to break the animal's neck.

But the mink struck too, and in the same instant as did the gander, and its sharp, little teeth put a half-moon wound across Duke's cheek. Then the little animal writhed briefly and was dead. Duchess walked over, and they talked in low tones, and Duke grasped the fur of the dead mink between his mandibles, and lifting, shook the animal as though to kill it again, and Duchess bowed approval and then invited him back into the shadow where the fading stars cast no light. But now he remained on guard, because what was between them was more than life. There was death too.

When Tom found the mink in the morning, he saw that Duchess had gone on her eggs. And, beginning then, Duke left the river often during daylight to fly low so his superbly sharp eye could probe into the shadowy barrel cave and he could know that all went well with Duchess.

The incubation went smoothly, and one warm morning

just as the dew was drying, the goslings, all armed with sharp egg openers on the ends of their tiny bills, began cracking shells, so that during the course of that day and the night which followed, they came limp and wet out onto the feathers with which the nest was lined to dry and lift their heads for a look at the world they'd been born into.

Only one infertile egg did not hatch, and Duchess thrust it from the nest with her bill, and when it was outside the nest she rolled it out of the barrel onto the hard-packed earth where Rank could find and dispose of it.

The first Saturday then, when Tom called in sick, Mack took the four downy goslings, all females, and their mother to the long, narrow field, and Duke joined them. While the five grazed, the gander stood tall and still as a statue, and with eyes which glistened in the sun watched for danger from the sky and the earth around.

And danger came, swift as a storm wind. In one instant the scene was one of pastoral peace, and in the next a whirl-wind of death was sweeping down on the geese. Mack jumped up shouting, but he might as well have asked the sun not to shine. There was no stopping the liver-and-white hunting dog once it had the hot scent of geese to trail on. A pup, never yet restrained or taught manners, swerved right on around Mack, and with its head and heart and every sinew pulsing with pursuit, came charging into the goose family.

Only Duke was alert enough to meet the attack. He charged with wings spread wide. But by the time he was flailing the dog with the bony-hard undersides of his powerful wings, the pup's jaws had already closed down across the

Duchess' neck, and she throttled herself and broke her own bones in a wild winging to escape.

The dog loosed its grip on the goose to turn on the gander. But before it could lash out there was blood running into its eyes, and terrified by the viciousness of the gander's attack, it turned yelping back to where the kennel door still swung back and forth and men were running and shouting.

But they were all too late for Duchess. She lay ruffled on the green grass, her neck at a grotesque angle from her beautiful body, and the frightened goslings had gathered around the gander.

Mack knelt beside the dead goose while Duke led his goslings to a safe distance, and when Duchess didn't follow, he made little noises in his throat for her to get up and come over.

So Mack gave them room. He got up and went to the farthest end of the field so Duke might find out, and when he was as far as the stone fence, the gander walked over, and putting out his neck, took a few feathers between his bill and tugged gently. Then he lifted his head and mourned once in a low and plaintive tone, and turning, walked away with the goslings in tow.

Mack did not try to stop them, and they walked to the end of the green field and down through the tall grass of a hay field to where the creek was silvery over a bottom of stony jewels and out into the little current which floated them—the gander and four goslings—under the white footbridge, through the enormous concrete culvert beneath the road, out onto the descending meadow, on down and down through willow and dogwood brakes to the Rose River.

Raising goslings required no special effort on the part of the gander. Unlike some of the drakes of the duck world which often join bachelor clubs once the hen refuses their advances, the Canada gander stays with and helps raise the family.

During incubation he guards the goose, and then when the goslings are born, he assumes parental duties in keeping with human standards. Thus endowed, Duke kept his family safe and together and led them to a back bay full of greens where there was a beach of sorts with gravel for the picking.

Mack came to visit them often, and though Duke swam his little gang into the rushes when he came, he was able to count them and be assured of their survival.

The goslings mushroomed into geese that summer, and their down became feathers, and the feathers lengthened to long, graceful fronds, and when the fronds were long and strong enough for skittering across the water in half-flight, Duke took to leaving them at intervals, and always he flew to the trout ranch and came low over the shed where Duchess had been penned, and he dipped down to the pond where he had taken her for a mate, and his wing tips almost touched his shadow when he flew the length of the long, green field where she had died.

And the men watched him, and Mack and Rank spoke of it sometimes, and they wondered if he did not know that Duchess was dead, or if it was that he just *had* to revisit the place where she had been his mate; if there was something within the gander which could neither be put down nor even understood and that down all the flyways of his life he would always remember and want to return to this place.

Then, when the goslings had learned to fly, they came with him on morning and evening flights, and though the youngsters were only aloft to strengthen their wings for the thousands of air miles they would be required to log, Duke always led them across the trout ranch, and the earthbound geese, whether envious or not, called out to them to come down, but they never did.

So the long, warm days shortened and cooled, and one night the browning grass was laid over by a silvery frost, and it took the sun until noon the next day to turn the white shine into glittering drops of water.

Duke was restless, and the youngsters perhaps caught the urgency from him, or from the lessening light, or from some ancient timing device beneath their short head feathers—and the daily flights took them farther afield, and now the youngsters talked incessantly until sometimes when heard from afar they sounded like a hound pack hunting the skyways.

Then, when the first wild packs came trumpeting out of the north, Duke called to them, and they called back, but the gander did not guide his flock up to where the others penciled their way south, nor did any of them come out of the sky to sample the hospitality of the back bay. They knew where they were going. They were all headed for Heron Marsh.

And now the maples on the hill were crimson, and in the river valley the willows were tawny. Now back by the ranch fence lines the oaks turned auburn, and nearer the water the birch were golden spears. Now the lily pads were tattered on the water which ran black under clouds more often than blue. Now the need.

And the need in Duke to go was as strong as the need he

felt to stay and fly low to the places of remembering. And he called out to the flocks which some days made endless procession on into the night. He wanted to go because he was a flocking bird. He needed to be a part of the procession like a bee must belong to a hive, and in the end to deny this heritage for a phantom mate who no longer called to him was as nigh impossible as it is impossible for a house plant to turn away from a window.

But he waited, and the crimson leaves of the maple turned ragged and brown and went spinning. The willow leaves were bright whorls on the wind. The birches were stripped bare, and a cold rain froze and then turned to snow, and when the sky cleared, scarves of white crowded around the new muskrat houses.

The youngsters, strong now and with feathers locked and as sleekly and steely gray as his, stayed but were wild with the need to go, and their entreaty to every passing flock was an almost incessant clamor.

Then one morning Duke lifted, and after a low swing over the trout ranch, began his ascent. The four young geese honked their approval as they lifted higher and higher, where there were stronger winds. In climbing they circled until they had come so high they could only see the earthbound flocks at the trout ranch as gray veins, like wind riffles on the water.

Then the upper airway claimed them, and when an updraft sent the little flock suddenly soaring, the youngsters whooped their joy. They spread their wing tips like fingers and beat the air rhythmically, arching their wings gracefully on the downbeat and straightening them to come back so they could be thrust down and back again.

Each air pocket was an adventure into which they plunged with the gaiety of children sliding down a rollercoaster. When a gust thrust them precipitously forward, they haronked with unbounded joy at moving so swiftly thousands of feet above the too solid earth.

Behind them were the cries of many geese, so Duke slowed the wing beat until a flock of more than a hundred drew alongside, and then they dropped into the slot on the abbreviated side of the lopsided V, and flying in the wing-tip vortex of the birds up ahead, moved easily at a speed which would take them hundreds of miles in a day.

Beneath, the earth slid north until the six ponds of the trout ranch were the merest pinpricks of light and the river a thread of dull silver. Duke turned his head once to look back. Never having joined in the noisy baying of the other birds, now he called out, but it was only a faint whisper of how perhaps he felt—and then the place was gone.

ON THE GROUND Mack and Rank had watched until the flock was a far-off speck in the sky. Then Rank turned to Mack. "Do you think he'll come back?" Rank asked.

Mack spread his hands, indicating that he didn't know. Then he said: "I doubt it. It was a freak thing that he came here in the first place. First off, he should have been mated months, or at least weeks, before he got this far north. Second, if a storm hadn't put the flock down, he'd never have met the goose. Third, it was nothing short of a miracle that *she* wasn't already mated. And fourth, the call to go north should have been stronger than the need to stay."

Both men were quiet for a while, then Rank asked: "Tell me, Mack, just what is known about the Canadas' mating habits?"

Mack thought for a minute and then he said: "Well, they used to think Canadas remained celibate if one or another lost its mate. Now they know that all of them don't. It's not easy to tell with wild birds, and captive birds change their habits, so that they're not a good indication of what really happens in the wilds."

"It's nice to think," Rank said, "that they mate for life and, maybe for the survivor, are even celibate after."

"Nice, but not very practical," Mack said.

"How do you mean?" Rank asked.

"Well," Mack said, "I've got a theory, and I've heard one or two biologists come up with the same theory, and that is that once all Canadas remained celibate after the death of a mate. The contention is that now, with hunting pressure taking such a terrific annual toll of birds, celibacy is such a risk to survival of the species that it has been abandoned."

The two men could hear the ducks talking softly and the occasional low plaint of one of the pinioned geese. They'd all be run into the poultry house soon. They wintered there because the ponds froze and it was easier to keep water available under a roof, where the temperature could be kept above freezing.

"Maybe he's even glad to be free," Rank said as they turned to walk back toward the ranch.

"Well, he won't be once the hunting season opens," Mack said. "Before the winter is over the poor old guy will probably wish a hundred times he had been born anything but a goose."

"I hope he makes it," Rank said.

Mack laughed. "At any rate he won't be plagued by thoughts of dying, and what's one goose more or less? They slaughter them by the tens of thousands every year, and tens of thousands more are born for the next year's killing. It's almost like managed mayhem."

Rank said nothing, and at the fork in the walk Mack went toward the house and Rank walked on down toward the hatchery. A pony snuffled. A trout broke water. A goose in the sky called down, and both men looked up at another V wedging its way south.

> ➤ ➤ ➤

*T*HE GREAT GOOSE FLOCK arrowed
south, and like children come to a party, Duke's youngsters
were infected with the gaiety of the gang and gabbled incessantly. Duke remained silent, flying expertly in the slip-
stream pocket of the goose ahead and making a place for the
daughter who followed behind. Several times he turned his
head as though looking back, but his wings never missed a
beat.

He did not join in the wild honking when Lake Winnebago slid into view and the flock could look down on the
smoldering city of Oshkosh stretching concrete tentacles south
to Fond du Lac and in every direction to lesser huddles of
houses marking small towns.

It was thrilling for the young geese to be so high with
all the world imprisoned below, and their exuberance was
something Gabriel might envy. On his first flight Duke had
been as excited as the rest of the first-year geese. But today
he displayed no emotion, and when an airplane heading for
Minneapolis cast its dull shadow over the flock and some of
the birds slid in and out of line, he kept the rhythm.

Of course, he had seen it all before: The rooftops and
the smoking chimneys and the fields with cattle looking like
insects. He had seen the cars committed to grinding out their

insides along winding trails. The people running, waving. The boats trailed by white plumes. The trains curling like snakes along twin rails. Sheep drifting like earthbound clouds. Horses running wild to their honking, manes and tails streaking. Flits of songbirds hedgehopping south. Knots of ducks in the air and rafts of ducks on the water. Poison clouds marking cities farther down the line of flight than they could see. A clutter. No plan, nor any pattern. Houses strewn like hailstones. Roads wrapping around onto themselves. No world of his, nor of any wild thing.

On and on until the first thin layer of night was like a gray veil, and then the V tipped forward like an airplane during descent, and each bird slowed the tempo. Wing beats became more measured. The earth pulled at them. And they were glad to give in, glad to lower along with scores of flocks converging from all northerly directions. Some of the geese called out because they had not eaten for a long time. Some flocks had come nonstop all the way south from Lake Superior, from a country where trees grew right out of rocks and the lakes were clear and deep and the rivers ran swiftly out of the hills.

Then from the earth came the first welcoming "haronk," and quickly another and another, until the babble became an incessant wind of sound and the descending flocks could see long ribbons of geese literally hiding the waters of the canals, wide swaths of gray-black birds covering the green fields, long furrows of geese moving restlessly between rows of corn stalks—thousands upon thousands.

The V in which Duke and his daughters were flying leveled off abruptly. Birds had to brake with their wings to keep from running one over the other. The formation disintegrated, and after a brief wild winging the geese began to spill wind from their wings. The birds sideslipped sharply and expertly from left to right, and right to left. Down sharply as kites which have lost the wind. Sideways. Straight. Sideways again. Scattering. Plummeting. Holding position. Dropping. Then the ground loomed and the geese braked hard to set themselves gently to earth.

Preen feathers gone awry. Stretch long necks. Walk and unlimber legs. Stand alert and listen. Look left and right and all around. The flock quieting gradually in the deepening dark. Only a few flocks left up where the light is brighter, calling out for landing instructions. Sentinels to their posts. Geese feeding. Geese drinking. Geese running water over their backs. Geese nibbling for a loose louse. Geese bobbing their heads. Geese stepping sedately.

Shelled corn bright even in the night all along the deep ruts of a road. Corn on cobs hanging from specially bred short stalks so the geese can reach them. Winter wheat. Long strips of lawn grass. Barren runts of trees killed by rising water. Thick stands of cattails. Round reeds smooth as pencils. Tattered pads and brown wrinkled prune seeds of the lily. Paradise. A goose paradise. A Canada goose paradise.

Once the land on which the tens of thousands of geese are sojourning was a seventeen-mile-long lake, five miles wide. Coal barges plied it. Excursion boats ran out of Heron. Fishermen set lines and nets. Hunting clubs built clubhouses on its shores to house the gunners when they weren't after ducks, both divers and the puddlers. But few geese came.

The waters were held in the lake by a dam at Heron, but

farmers said it put water up into their fields. Investors laying claim to lake bottom joined the farmers. The dam was destroyed. The waters bled away. The lake became a great sea of rough, tough marsh grass.

Fires, started in order to grow thicker grass for more hay, sometimes burned year around, but especially in fall, and the smoke went on the prevailingly westerly wind all the sixty miles to Milwaukee, and the people there held their noses and said: "Heron Marsh is burning again."

And only assorted small wild things like rabbits and juncos and a few jays or some families of skunks plus a few frogs and a casting of grasshoppers lived on the marsh.

It was a seedless sea of infertility in summer and a white waste with seldom a bush to break the snow in winter—almost all the way from Winston south to Heron; and all the way from the low hills to the east to the railroad tracks and Highway 56 to the west. And it was such a dead place that in winter the only sign of life came from the railroad, where engines spit sparks and soot darkened the snow.

Some few were beguiled by its flat, treeless and rockless promise, but they took few crops from the sour soil where peat fires burned ten-foot hells into the ground, and in the end a few men of money bought it up for pennies the acre and cut the rasping hay for packing dishes, wine and bric-a-brac.

But there were some who had remembered how it was, and among them were such men as envisioned what it might again be, so a feud was begun between the men who wanted packing hay and those who wanted a place where all wild things could come.

In the end the conservationists won out, and a new dam was built, and it was a more manageable structure, so water levels might be controlled, and instead of a lake there were potholes and puddles and ponds and canals and long, wide and wet marshes. So the peat fires went out, and the geese came.

There were only a few at first, so a captive flock was kept to tempt them. Then more and more came, until finally tens of thousands knew its precise location. With the geese came the ducks and all manner of cranes and herons, tens of thousands of blackbirds, and also the bright-eyed marsh wren, gallinules and coots, rails and snipes, plovers and chickadees, hawks and sometimes eagles—every feathery family, until there was no other place on the continent except the Florida Everglades which so teemed with birds.

And deer came too, and raccoons and opossums and foxes and mink and rabbits and so many thousands of muskrats that men left their regular jobs to get permits to put out traps.

Fish came too. Bullheads and northern pike and perch and sometimes walleyes swam the branches of the Stone River, and there were carp and minnows for any living thing like kingfishers or coons.

And the politicians kept their promise and made one-half of the wildlife reservoir into a refuge while the other half was managed for hunters, and they came to Heron from Washington on dedication day, and the speaker vowed: "No man shall ever carry a gun on these acres. This is an inviolate refuge. It is ours to keep in trust."

It was a good and noble speech, and the man meant it, but

either he was naïve or maybe only ignorant of the greed of his fellow man.

THIS WAS THE PLACE, then, the trap, if you will, where Duke and his daughters grazed, and even before they came to the canal they had full crops, and when they swam across to where the corn was, they had room for only a few kernels. So they swam again, and coming to a muskrat house, decided to make camp. All five climbed from the water to the roof of the house still in the process of being built, and when the muskrats came back with moss in their teeth and cattails dragging behind in the water, Duke put out his neck and warned them off. The 'rats floated out a little way to where the gander could not reach them to ponder on this intrusion.

And then they moved along, and although they had nearly completed the house from which the geese had evicted them, they started another, because the days were short and now they were impelled to work, and perhaps tomorrow they would come back to the nearly finished house if the geese had gone.

Duke lifted a leg and locked the other, and putting his beak to his feathers, rested. But the youngsters could not sleep because of the excitement of the place, and they came off and on the house to swim and drink and eat green tendrils, until at last they slept, floating on the water.

Next morning a golden haze filtered the sun's light to begin an Indian-summer day of silken floss floating, and with frogs back up out of the mud and turtles on their logs. It was a rare respite, a time for songbirds to fluff in the luxury of a dust bath.

Duke stretched and craned his neck before coming down

off the muskrat house for a short swim, a brief bath and a long drink. Then he led the goslings to where he could see a drift of corn just dumped by a growling truck. As the vehicle progressed, it winnowed geese into the air, but they dropped right back in the ruts along its route.

Duke's daughters followed in single file, and when they saw such a prosperity of corn they haronked anxiously and walked a little faster to come past him and eat greedily for a few seconds. Their first hunger satisfied, they became more picky and took the plump kernels first.

All crops full, Duke led the way to the canal bank, and they searched for little stones to help grind the food in their gizzards, and then they rested.

Now the first excitement of the staging area was over, and Duke and his daughters felt a part of the armada. So they lolled all morning like vacationers at a summer resort, and after noon they tried a little more corn and sipped some water.

Goose families were leaving the marsh now. They went out in low sweeps to swing over the farmlands which came down to the marsh from all sides. Most were first-year non-breeders and those families which had never used the staging area and wanted a look around. Sometimes youngsters of the year could not stay still and almost literally talked the old geese into taking them for a flight.

Duke's four daughters were restless, so he turned into the light breeze, and running lightly on the canal, hit the air with his breast and with wings pushing took off at a long slant for altitude. The youngsters followed.

Duke went east to where the hills were higher and he could ride small thermal lifts, and the daughters yelped like children just loosed from school. But Duke spoke to them and they stayed in line, a file of five geese, and in the sunlight their white throat scarves and rump patches gleamed as they sought out air currents and followed them.

On some green fields they saw goose flocks, and though they called to them, they did not go down. They flew as far as Marionville, turned south and west and came to Heron and then followed the highways to Rousteau. Over Rousteau they turned back toward Stone River and then went south on the river to Lake Bluestone, with its islands and the town lying where the lake spilled its guts over a dam and thundered for a ways to become quiet and snaky between bankside trees.

Where a field of winter wheat stretched down to the water, Duke circled. He climbed a hundred yards higher so he could see more of the area surrounding the field. Then without a sound he guided the youngsters directly to the center of the flat field, where he might see danger from any direction.

While the daughters snipped selectively at the short stems of winter wheat, he stood motionless. After the youngsters had eaten, the largest of the four stood guard while Duke ate.

The sun was getting low when Duke turned west, and taking the little breeze under his wings, lifted. He flew almost straight north over fertile farm fields and pockets of swamp and patches of woods, over networks of gravel roads until he came back to where the river turned. The sun was down by the time he came over Heron and began his letdown to the marsh.

Duke landed his family before dark, where the muskrats were back at work roofing their house. Duke sent the 'rats diving and climbed out of the water. His daughters floated in front of him.

Everything seemed the same, but there was a feeling of uneasiness in the air, and Duke complained about it. Other geese felt it too, and they gabbled softly. As darkness deepened, noises from around the perimeter of the marsh intruded to the places where the geese were sleeping. There were lights along all the roads. Small airplanes went buzzing over. A gun went off, and it seemed a hundred farm dogs barked.

Every sound was sharp because the cloying warmth of the Indian-summer day had given way to a crisp night of brilliant starlight. Sometimes shrill shouting came down into the marsh as exuberant hunters built bonfires along the road.

There was the occasional fight as one or another laid claim to a hilltop hunting blind which was not his, and then the farmer had to get out of bed and come down to settle which man it was had paid him the ten dollars to shoot from that point of vantage the next day.

But the farmer settled nothing, because the geese heard the dispute resume when he'd gone off to bed.

Game wardens drove the back roads, and deputy sheriffs drove along Highway 56 to corral speeders.

Some few cars were hopelessly stuck in ditches, and one auto overflowing with hunters was wrapped around a tree, and then an ambulance came screaming out of the flatland from Beaver Dam, and it was a piercing and nerve-rending sound for the geese. The sound seemed to go on forever, wailing from far off and then coming closer, and then departing but still heard on and on—a thin scream in the night.

All night they came like the gathering of a great army for a momentous assault, until an entire division had been deployed five deep and twenty deep, and off and across southern and central Wisconsin the reserves picked any point of vantage where a tired goose might try for a landing, until the land literally bristled with guns and the fields and streams and marshes and knolls were armed camps. And perhaps the geese had a feeling of being surrounded and cut off from escape to anywhere, because throughout the night they moved restlessly, and at intervals one or another distraught bird raised its voice, and then a ripple of consternation would run through the whole great flock.

Then, at an hour before dawn, men of the first firing line —who had been selected at a drawing held by the state— were issued arm bands to show that they were of the elite and privileged to take the first shot when the geese came out. Two by two, then, guns in one hand and vacuum bottles in the other, they marched down the roads to position themselves right in the refuge itself.

The blinds were placed at intervals of one hundred yards, so there was little chance a low-flying goose could get through the barrage. It was an impenetrable ring, and now that the last loop of the human noose had been drawn tightly around, the geese began to call out and to lift nervously for a short flight, only to drop back down again.

In the blinds the men settled themselves to await zero hour. They poured coffee into plastic cups and let the steam warm their faces. They lighted one cigarette after another and conversed in low tones, as though to keep secret their hiding place so the geese would not hesitate to fly close.

Among them were men who remembered how hunting was once such a sport that men spent days building concealments within the earth, and with nearly frozen fingers made such a placement of decoys as might entice a passing flock. In those days the Canada goose had been a trophy bird, and if one was killed it was a credit to the hunter for having outwitted it.

Not many men hunted Canadas then, because the challenge was too much for them and they were not willing to learn such skills with the call as could make a lead goose turn its flock into the fields where they were pitted.

These old-timers, each time they participated in a mass attack, swore they would never come back. But some kept coming, because there were no other places to hunt and they could not get the need to hunt out of their blood. Perhaps they always hoped it wouldn't be quite as terrible as it always was, that they'd find a place apart where only the redwing and the bright-eyed wren would share their secret.

In that hour before dawn it seemed the geese, aided by some extrasensory power of perception, felt in their vitals the grave danger of their predicament, and if they had no way of realizing the nature of the threat, they seemed deeply disturbed. Some especially nervous parents from this group or that took their families aloft and flew across the lines looking down at the dim forms huddled close to the earth. In the dark the men could hear the sharp rip of their wings, and here and there a goose cried out a warning as one hunter or another foolishly turned a flashlight skyward in hopes of silhouetting the passing flock.

And the geese were not the only ones disturbed. Hunters

who had moved into the state side of the marsh, where hunting was legal but no geese lived, frightened whole rafts of ducks from the water. These went hurtling north to the place of refuge where the geese were. Green and blue-wing teal, mallards, shovelers, widgeon, ringbills—family flocks and larger concentrations en route to wintering grounds moved across the bending grasses to the federal side of the marsh.

Herons and bitterns and cranes, frightened from their night camps, squawked in alarm as they lifted to look for less crowded acres. Blackbirds, thick as swarming bees, churned up out of the cattails and flew blindly, to swirl back down again.

Coots deserted the open water for the protection of the reeds. Raccoons out for a pre-dawn stroll scurried to their hollow trees. The little rails hurried back and forth like water bugs. Deer, frightened from the willow bluffs, ran out onto the farmers' fields, only to be frightened back into the brakes again.

And still the hunters came, and a hundred and a thousand flashlights stabbed the night. A hundred, a thousand boots pounded down off the roads and squished through the wet places where the bottomlands began.

More and more cars came. They moved back and forth along the narrow roads, their drivers searching hopefully for a place to hunt. Finding no place left, men merely parked their cars, determined to hunt from the road.

There were traffic jams on dirt lanes meant only for manure spreaders. There were harsh words. Gates were left open, and cattle strayed. Wires were cut, and sheep wandered down the roads, scattering before the headlights of cars. Autos jammed farmers' yards.

Where a tavern stood on a rise along Highway 69, which intersects the northern end of the marsh, thirty hunters waited for the door to open. And still they came out of restaurants and hotels and motels and homes in Oshkosh, Fond du Lac, Heron, Marionville, Beaver Dam, Brandon, New Holstein, Milwaukee, Columbus, Sun Prairie—twenty, thirty, forty towns—all late and hurrying to hunt where there were no places to hunt, coming like locusts to kill a goose, wanting to be first, lest the geese become wary and refuse to fly out.

They walked from the highway down along the railroad until they were like an infantry line planning to go over the top. Sometimes they were almost elbow to elbow. Car radios played, and heaters hummed, and the men smoked cigarettes and drank coffee and the noise of it all came down out of the low hills like an ominous threat to where the geese were trapped.

Then came the first streak of light in the east, and with it an explosion of guns to the south. There was a second streak of light and explosions to the north, and a game warden said: "Damn them! It isn't time yet!"

Then the east broke open into a long pink crater, and then no living thing—furred or feathered—was safe at Heron Marsh.

> ➤ ➤ ➤ ➤

*A*s WAS THEIR HABIT, the geese be-
gan morning flights at dawn, and lead like a blizzard swept
the perimeter of the marsh. Armadas of geese wilted, and the
voices of terrified birds was a thin violin string of sound across
the drum beat of guns. They fell like flies caught in a lethal
spray.

Birds with broken wings plummeted. Geese absorbing
fatal body shots set their wings and sailed to burst their breasts
on the hard ground. Some came down like rags. Others turned
end over end, craning their necks. Geese climbed and dived
and sailed and fell in every conceivable aerial attitude as
flocks disintegrated.

Some families rallied, only to be blown apart again. Distraught geese followed fallen mates straight into the guns.

For fifteen minutes shots crackled like the sound of a fire
running through a forest. Then it was as though the geese
remembered and the shooting diminished and there were only
sporadic explosions, as among the ashes when the fire has
passed.

The great mass of geese settled back into the refuge. Except for the persistently mournful cries of widow and widower,
the flock was mostly silent. Only the single geese remained
aloft, reluctant to end their search. And sometimes confused

youngsters, with no parents to guide them, flew into the guns.

Even the blackbirds, so prone to swirl, stayed down. Ducks did not hedgehop to puddle-visit. And the usually imperturbable wrens sat as though shocked into silence. The concussion of sound had been so overwhelming the wild society seemed stunned by it.

Even the men themselves—in the blinds, on the hills, along the roads, in the pits, along the fence rows, behind the cars—were silent as witnesses to a funeral. It took the hunters twenty minutes to regain their combined composure after the assault. Then first one and then another tried to call the geese out by blowing on goose calls. But no goose accepted the invitation, because the callers were almost hilariously human.

Inside the refuge the wounded tried to fathom the wing that wouldn't work, the leg that dangled, the burning and biting in the breast, neck and thigh. Some sat sick and disheveled on ditch banks. Others crawled among the reeds, and stretching their necks, died.

Duke and his daughters had come down off the rotting muskrat house to swim about nervously. The gander had not taken his family into the air. He only watched and listened, and though he could not understand the danger, he knew where the firing line lay.

Most of the Canadas, being a breed of highly perceptive birds, also knew now that to cross a given line would precipitate an explosion. So they settled for what they had and ate the corn and grass and drank from the canals and slept on the water and on the banks and knolls and logs and muskrat houses. Perhaps they didn't know it, but they could have waited out the hunters until freeze-up time if necessary, and by that time the hunting season in the northern zone would have ended and they could continue their trip south.

But the hunters were not happy. Angered at the reluctance of the geese to come out and be killed, they began shouting to one another about how poor hunting was. The impatient ones came from their hiding places and sat in the sun to smoke cigarettes and eat sandwiches and drink coffee from vacuum bottles. Car motors roared and warmed so men could put their hands to the heaters, and then the first autos began stringing down off the high places to head toward home, because nowhere was there a goose in the sky.

In the afternoon a breeze came up and a half-dozen flocks lifted on it, and whether they had forgotten or thought the siege had been lifted, tried to cross the firing line. But hunters still waited, and some geese were killed and others wounded, and the rest came back. Then a somnolence settled over the marsh, and hunters and geese alike slept or moved lazily to nibble at tendrils, or in the case of hunters, smoke cigarettes or drink coffee.

When the sun set, the army of hunters lifted like ants from a gigantic hill and began moving in every direction. Car lights came on. Horns sounded raucously down into the marsh. Men shouted. Scores stopped at the conservation department checking stations, and attendants there heard angry complaints about how the geese were being fed so well they would not come out to be shot, and what good was there in a man spending money for a hunting license if the geese did not come out to be killed.

That night there were telephone calls to the state conservation commissioners and to the governor and to the refuge manager. Some even called Washington, D.C., to tell their congressmen how their hunting was being sabotaged by feeding the geese within the refuge, and how could they get any hunting that way?

The politicians listened. They were concerned. Hundreds of thousands of hunters throughout the state added up to a lot of votes. Moneys paid by them for hunting and fishing licenses virtually financed the state's conservation efforts. The three-dollar federal duck stamp annually brought in hundreds of thousands of dollars. Tens of thousands of people owed their jobs to the men who came with guns and the people who came with fishing rods. The politicians could not ignore them.

But next day the trucks rolled again from the warehouses, and corn was spilled for geese to eat, and except for a few waves of foolish first-year birds which came to the firing line at sunup, the hunters had nothing to shoot at.

Occasionally during the day the odd goose, or the odd gander, still hopeful of finding its mate, flew too low over the guns and went down, but when night came not twenty geese, out of the tens of thousands in the refuge, had been killed. Some hunters were so angry they vowed to invade the refuge itself if the feeding did not stop.

The pressure on the refuge manager became intolerable. There were investors who had paid exorbitant prices for farms from which they had hoped to make a killing renting goose blinds. Wealthy hunters with much frontage on the marsh had invited important guests, hoping to provide them with an exciting hunt. Thousands of workers had postponed summer vacations so they could spend their two or three weeks in a goose blind along the fringe of the refuge. Hundreds had given up beer and bowling so they might have a fine shotgun, a hunting coat, high rubber boots.

Then, when the crowds coming to Heron, Winston and other towns around began to dwindle, the restaurant and tavern owners felt the pinch, the motel and hotel owners put up vacancy signs, the gas-station attendants sat idle, and they began to add their voices to the mounting clamor.

So one day a call came through to the marsh manager: "Stop feeding the geese!"

So no trucks rolled the next day, but there still was an abundance of food. But when no corn was spread on the second, third and fourth days, the leavings had been picked over, and the grass was all but cropped, and the armada of geese, which had grown to one hundred and twenty thousand birds, was eating any edible thing and becoming hungrier with every passing hour.

Duke felt the pinch, but he led his family into back bays where grass along the water's edge still hadn't been plucked, and he found them seeds fallen into the muck and snails and worms, and though it wasn't enough, it kept up their strength, and though they took short flights within the refuge, he did not lead his little flock near the firing line.

It wasn't until the sixth day that the hungry geese began going out. First a scattering of flocks, and, clawing for altitude, some of the birds got through.

Though the hunters were perfectly within their rights, the press of their numbers was just too much for the geese. Once past the firing line they had to contend with the hunters on private lands. Men shot at them from hills, along roads and pitted in corn and winter-wheat fields. There was no place to land, and the shooting pushed the geese higher and higher, but even then the odd pellet from a high-powered ten-gauge magnum gun got through to find a vital spot in a long neck, a wing tip . . . and some geese came down.

Nevertheless, geese kept filtering out of the marsh throughout the day. It was becoming imperative that they find food, and if the refuge did not provide it, they necessarily had to fly out to look for it.

Duke did not try to cross the firing line, though the youngsters complained loudly. He toured the canals with them in tow, walked from puddle to puddle, flew to the knolls and the ridges . . . finding a little grass, some acorns, seeds fallen and on the stem. . . .

During the night a south wind brought unseasonably warm weather, and the cold ground breathed up a solid covering of fog. Day came gradually, almost imperceptibly. Visibility had been cut to the killing range of a shotgun. Hunters were completely hidden by it. Goose flocks nearly collided in lifting. The birds found the flying difficult because of the density of the air mass. It was like winging through cotton, yielding but cloying, and the speed with which the flock could lift was cut by half. But the enfolding fog gave the birds a false sense of security, and they started going out.

Duke decided to risk it, to make a run for the green field they had visited the day before the shooting started. Going out, he stayed close to the ground to sight on any familiar landmark, and came winging into the firing line hardly a hundred feet high.

The family of five heard the sizzle of lead cutting through their flock even before they heard the gun blast. One youngster's leg was hit and dangled and another called out as pellets lodged against its heavy breastbone.

Duke turned, and they sailed back into the refuge. But other geese hoping to get through in the fog were not so easily dissuaded, and thousands came to the line, where thousands of men waited. The hunters had only shadows to shoot at, but they kept up an incessant barrage, and geese died by the hundreds, and hundreds more were crippled.

Confused in the fog because they could not readily know where the firing line was, geese milled around and around, coming time and again over the guns, and many were knocked from the sky, but in the low overcast the hunters never knew they had fallen. Families were wiped out. Ganders became widowers. Geese became widowed.

Still the geese, disoriented, kept coming to the line, and even Duke, after flying low along the cattail tops, decided to try again. But this time he gained altitude before coming to the perimeter, and when he moved out of the marsh he was so high the hunters below did not know he had passed his flock over them.

Duke angled upward, away from the sound of guns and wounded geese, higher and higher, to a point where the fog began to thin out. Then they broke through into brilliant sunlight, and the fog lay below, shining white. Other goose flocks had made it. Some ducks had come out too.

Duke flew a wide circle, and when the two wounded ones lagged, he slowed his pace. He flew until the sun melted away the fog beneath, and then took a heading on the river. He followed it south to Lake Bluestone, and above the village of Harriford he could see the green field a mile south. He started his descent at the edge of town, and the youngsters gabbled anxiously as they saw the lush winter wheat.

Down, down . . . just topping the trees to slide around and into the wind to prepare for a mid-field landing. At the last instant Duke saw the danger, and he called out a warning and beat frantically to climb back to safety. But the youngsters had not noticed the disturbed earth, and when the camouflaged trap door of a pit flew back and guns came squirting out, they were already on the ground.

The goose with the wounded leg had trouble getting back into the air, and she died first. Then a second goose caught a charge of number-two shot full in the breast and sailed off to land in the high grass near the river. A third goose caught some pellets in the fleshy part of her thigh but managed to climb despite them.

Then, while one of the hunters ran to where the goose was threshing in the long grass, Duke brought his two remaining youngsters up to altitude, and when they turned north he could see the man beating the dying goose with a stick until it lay still and only its wings quivered a little.

Duke's course took him back to the river, and he flew the eight miles from Harriford to Log Bridge and then back again. He scanned the river to see if there were some place he might land and dip in a back bay for water weeds to fill his shrinking crop.

Twice he went low, only to spot hunters hidden in the rushes, and honking with alarm, he climbed back to a safe altitude. Finally he turned east and flew over Slinger and Hartford, and then going north to avoid Milwaukee, came to Lake Michigan.

At three thousand feet he could see the smokes of Port Washington to the north, and Milwaukee and Racine to the south. Below he could see the waves break, to send white foam rinds skimming up onto the sand. Out ahead a large ore boat moved ponderously ahead of an insignificant tassel of black smoke. Closer to shore a single tug plowed the blue water on the way to port.

There were rafts of ducks, mostly bluebills, lifting and falling like slate-colored islands. Their presence signaled safety, and tired now because of his long fast, and with the wounded one complaining, he let down until the three geese were bobbing on the waves a short distance from a raft of ducks.

It was restful on the water. There was an almost hypnotic rhythm to the lifting and falling waves. Here, far from land, there was no danger, but neither was there any food.

But the ducks were feeding. They dived thirty feet to the bottom for mollusks, and then on the way up snipped some salad from a submerged weed bed. But the geese did not know about diving. They were primarily land birds, even though they had webbed feet and water-resistant feathers.

It was not like Duke to move among the ducks. Between ducks and geese there are no amenities. If they do not actually hate one another, they are loath to mingle. But when Duke saw the ducks were eating, he swam his two daughters nearer. The ducks edged away, and Duke, with the need for food a numbing necessity, swam right among them to scavenge for scraps of vegetation which had floated to the surface.

It was a godsend. In tearing off bite-size pieces for them-selves, the ducks sometimes uprooted whole plants and they came to the surface to spread their greenery to the sun. It was fine feeding for the three geese, and they followed along after the duck pack, picking up every scrap until their crops were full. Then, for no apparent reason and without any visible signal, the ducks all began to walk on the water with their stubby wings beating a tattoo against a strengthening wind. Seconds after they were airborne, the flock of bluebills disappeared over the horizon.

Duke and his youngsters rested then with their necks folded back, but they did not sleep. The sun went down and the wind picked up speed, until they were riding a galloping sea, and then when it was full dark, Duke permitted the waves to take them ashore. When he felt the sand beneath his webs, he walked up onto the beach out of reach of the breakers.

Here he stood for several minutes listening, but when there was no sound except the wash of waves, he relaxed. The youngster with the pellets in her thigh sank down and picked at the sand to see if there were bits of gravel in it. The other goose walked the shore looking for abrasive bits to help her grind her food.

Duke stood for an hour without moving, and then when it was black dark except for the stars overhead and the stars glinting like flint chips off the waves, he began to eat gravel.

Having found enough, he went back to the two geese, and then, turning into the wind, they settled on their webs. In a short time the wind had whipped little sand barriers around them, and they slept comfortably and without fear.

In the morning the wounded one couldn't walk. Where she had picked at the feathers along her thigh to bite away the pain, the flesh had turned green. Duke could smell the wound, and the puncture marks in the skin were oozing. Followed by his one unmarked daughter, Duke went into the water and swam out a little way. Then they waited. Several times the wounded goose scrambled to her one good leg, only to go careening over, and with wings fumbling for a hold on the wind, she went tumbling a little way down the beach.

The wounded goose's efforts to get back into the water caught the attention of a woman in a beach house back where higher ground lifted to a timbered slope. She called her husband, and he came with binoculars.

"By God, a goose!" he said, handing her the glasses and going for his gun.

When the man came running, Duke sounded the alarm, and he and the able daughter took to the air, but the wounded one only flopped along until a charge from the gun blasted her into the sand.

The man picked up the disheveled goose, and walking to the house, proudly displayed it as though he had shot a trophy.

"Meat on the table," the woman said, and her husband smiled.

Duke took his only remaining daughter so far out over the lake that land was only a blur. Then he skimmed down to to the waves, and they rested. Again they were in a safe place, but hunger was insistent, and there was nothing, because the patrolling gulls had scouted out every last edible scrap. So their only hope of survival was the land.

Duke lifted, and the young goose followed, and he went to five hundred feet so the passing duck flocks were below, and on sighting an island of goldeneyes, he coasted down to scavenge among them. But they were diving down to turn over stones for mollusks, and there were no water weeds, so the two geese found nothing.

But they stayed, hoping the diving ducks would turn up one leaf, one stem, one tendril. Then, when the goldeneyes lifted to look for other feeding grounds, the geese went to the air too.

Hopefully Duke glided down to another raft of ducks. But these, instead of being loosely flocked like all the others, swam in straight military lines, diving and surfacing in unison. They never broke their formation, because they were mergansers and they were fishing, and by keeping a tight formation they could keep a school of little fish on the run in front of them until each duck had caught one. So once again there was nothing.

Noon whistles rent the air, and the mergansers flew away. Duke lifted, and the goose followed, and going to a thousand feet, they headed back for the marsh. At least on the marsh there would be something, if only wire grass or rotting cattail stalks, or an insect or a small fish—poor goose fare, but something to live on.

He came to the river below Heron and flew north. Coming near the marsh edge, he made a swift descent. It was a mistake. With the first blast, Duke's one remaining daughter went flopping from the sky. Instead of climbing to get out of range, the gander followed her down. He saw the water fly when she splatted in a puddle. Then he felt lead take him in the heavy breast meat. He winged frantically for altitude. Again he felt pellets pound his breast. Then he was over the firing line, and coming above the massed geese, he glided down.

When he dumped into the ditch, he drank even before he had planed to a halt, and then climbing the bank, he stood and picked at the place where the pellets had penetrated his breast. Two of the pellets just beneath the skin were pecked free and dropped. Four other pellets, the size of apple seeds, had buried themselves too deeply to be dug out. Except for a few tiny drops on his gray breast, there was almost no bleeding.

He spent the night alternately searching for food and sleeping. At dawn he was awakened by the crackle of guns running again like fire up and down and around the perimeter of the marsh. Now he felt no need for food. There was an intense burning in his breast. He crept to the crown of an old muskrat house, where there was some heat from the rotting moss below, and sat soaking sunrays.

As the day progressed a film came over his eyes, and from time to time he walked weakly to the edge of the house to drink water. The burning which had been localized in his breast now spread to his entire body. He let his wings droop, and when his feathers went awry he did not ruffle and preen them back into place, but remained disheveled.

Night came, but Duke did not know it. He was too sick to go for water. He laid out his long neck in the manner of a goose dying, and if any cared, it could only have been the stars, because there was no one else to see.

In the morning he was all but dead. He lifted his head, but he could not hold it erect, so he stretched it far enough forward to bring him off balance. That way he tumbled off the soggy moss-and-cattail house into the water.

He drank, and his eyes cleared a little. As though from a

great distance, he could again hear the guns and the cries of distraught geese.

Listlessly he paddled to the bank and nibbled at some soggy, rotting grass. Once a goose, which had been going from flock to flock searching for her mate, swam up to him. She looked him over and then swam on.

The sunset was red in his eyes, but he never saw it. He found the muskrat house but was unable to climb back onto it. His head came lower and lower, until it was resting on the water. He paddled feebly into an inlet between rushes, and on a cattail wand which had been laid over by the wind, he rested his head.

> ↣ ↣ ↣ ↣ ↣

QUITE ABRUPTLY, then, the shooting ceased. The season had ended. Duke was only vaguely aware that an unusual stillness had settled over the marsh. After spending the night for the most part unconscious on the water, he had revived enough the next morning to pull himself to the top of the muskrat house. In his emaciated condition his body was not manufacturing enough oil, and he was not strong enough to slick what there was around to waterproof his feathers, and to remain in the ditch might mean sinking to the bottom.

Now even the great mass of geese was uncommonly quiet. The marsh manager had ordered that feeding be resumed, and the trucks once again crawled along the slippery roads to dump bright-orange kernels on the islands.

Only the widows and the widowers flew from place to place looking. Of each flock they inquired. And when every flock had been visited, they flew back to the place they had last seen their mates and started searching anew. A few might go on searching to the end of their days. And every time the flock with which they joined came to a new place of strange birds, they would go through the entire gaggle, hoping that perhaps among these the lost would be found.

Duke was beyond caring. His life was guttering. Burning

with fever, he only moved to the edge of the rotting 'rat house to take water, and then back to where he could lie with his neck stretched before him.

A day, two days, and then three slipped away, and to the gander they passed as a blur, first sunlight then stars, then sunlight again. . . . He lost so much weight that his breastbone was a sharp protrusion parting the breast feathers to the left and to the right. The rims of his eyes were ringed with yellow pus, and sometimes after he had slept, he had difficulty in breaking the seal of mucus so that he could discern daylight from dark.

On the fourth day he should have died, but the strong heart which can send a Canada goose down the airways a thousand miles through wind-ripped skies kept beating, and then the corpuscles of healing began winning the battle for life, and blood in the gander's veins cooled.

On the fifth morning Duke awakened clear of eye and brain, but so weak that he had to push with webs and wings to get into the water. Floating on the surface of the ditch, he tried to lift his head, but managed to get it only high enough to rest his beak for support on the edge of the muskrat house.

When the wave of weakness caused by the effort needed to get into the water had passed, he nibbled at the rotting moss and managed to swallow some. He closed his eyes and rested. When he opened them again he spotted a vividly green patch of duckwort floating where the muskrats had laid a trail among the rushes. Head low, he swam and skimmed the tiny floating plants up with his bill so they trickled with the water into his throat, and he swallowed them.

There was a dead minnow, soft with rot. He ate it. There

were two snails, and he swallowed them. Some muskrat dung, and he ate that too. Propelling himself with his wings because his webs weren't yet strong enough, he came to a muskrat feed bed and frightened off the animal. Shreds of green floated where the muskrat had feasted. He ate them all, carefully, so none was missed.

By nightfall he had found enough to give him strength for lifting his head, and then he swam to the islands where the corn had been dumped. But he did not gorge, because something within him warned against it. He ate sparingly and then went to the edge of the water to flop down on his webs to sleep.

All night he heard geese calling. He heard their wings cutting the air. He saw the shadows of their flocks passing. Then in the morning there was ice where the water had been, and all that was left of the great goose gathering were scattered flocks stringing along the main flow of the river where the current had kept it open.

Duke pecked at the ice tentatively, and then turning, went back to where the corn was. After filling his crop, he walked slowly out onto the ice and along the ditch until he came to a wide canal. He followed the canal until he came to the river, where he joined a small gathering of geese where water was a black cut in the bright ice.

After drinking, he went to the canal banks to look among the brittle frozen grasses for tiny stones. He had not replenished his gizzard supply since being wounded, and the corn was lumping up in his crop because his gizzard could not get on with the job of grinding it up for energy. He found enough, and then sinking to the ground, was warm in the sun, though the temperature dropped steadily, and by nightfall even the current in the river was not enough to stay the ice.

That night the last of the geese left, and now he was the only one, and in the morning when he could find no open water, he ate the frost which had whitened the dried grass along the ditch bank. After eating, he tried to fly.

He ran, beating his wings frantically, but they lacked thrust. He was not strong enough to free himself of the earth, and in the end he went tumbling like a big, broken toy.

So he walked, looking for water, and sometimes he called out plaintively, perhaps for his goslings, perhaps for his goose.

In the afternoon he went to where there still was corn and ate some. After that he continued his search for water. Toward evening he came to a protected place in the lee of an island where muskrats had opened an air hole. He sat on the edge of the hole and drank. Then, unwilling to leave the place, he slept.

That night the wind went around into the northeast, and snow came. Big flakes fell softly as breast feathers. But the wind would not let them rest. Lifting the snow, the wind drove it into drifts, and Duke had to stand and shake often to keep from being covered.

The snow stopped falling at dawn, but now the marsh was desolate. Only its iced veins glistened. Its islands were impassable snow hummocks with skeletons of reaching trees. The marshes were dry bones of cattails rattling. The fields of alfalfa and rye and winter wheat were barren white raceways.

No furred or feathered thing moved in the shadow and shine of wind-carved drifts. But most tragic of all, the corn had been covered.

Duke floundered through the snow, to come back to the windswept ice of the river. Through the ice he saw the white belly of a dead fish. From a snow bank the wing of a dead goose protruded, and the feathers fluted in the wind. Muskrats were only bubble trails beneath the ice apron. But he kept walking until he came to the canal, back to the ditch, and finally to the island where he had eaten the corn. But he could not broach the drifts. Hurling himself, he landed in the soft snow and was trapped. Only his wings, spread on either side, kept him from sinking. By arching his neck he could turn, until he was facing the ditch. Then, with a frenzy of winging he got back onto the ice.

Then he rested and looked around, and it was inconceivable that the place had once been the site of riotous birdsongs of spring, the throbbing insect orchestra of summer, and the wing beat of the big birds in fall.

The marsh seemed forlorn, sleeping soundly, almost dead. Who could ever believe now that redwings once bent the rushes, herons swirled above rookeries, bitterns pumped and coots complained? By what stretch of the imagination could anyone understand that the marsh was neither dead nor even sleeping, but only waiting for the time to again be the beginning of life—that someday again the turtles and frogs would come out of their mud holes, the insect eggs would hatch and the air would hum, and then flock by flock such a myriad of birds would converge on the green acres that to even count them would be impossible.

What promise was there now that her breast would give life to millions?

The gander shook to free his feathers of snow. Then he started to trek south, and he kept to the ditches and the canals and followed one and then another tiny gut, where little frozen streams came down from the hills, until there was a black plowed field swept clean of snow.

He walked between the frozen furrows, and the dark earth absorbed the sunlight and small puddles furnished water, but there was no food.

After drinking, he tried his wings again, but he had lost too much flesh, and the powerful breasts, which were all muscle, were still too string thin, and though he could feel his feet come off the ground, he was not strong enough to become airborne.

So he rested, and while resting, heard the far-off gabble of geese. He started in the direction of the sound but then stopped. They were not of his kind, these geese talking. He had never heard the language. Yet he knew they were geese.

And where there were geese, or any other bird, something told him there would be food, so he walked past the pits where the gunners had waited.

It was like coming across a battlefield months after the war. Red hulls of spent shotgun shells were the mementos. And he passed a mitten, black and woolly, hanging on the barbs of a fence. He pecked at the filter ends of discarded cigarettes. The shine of a discarded vacuum bottle caught his eye. There was tissue paper, soggy and pink and white and blue.

The gabble of the geese was louder, and then Duke

stopped. The sound was coming from a grouping of buildings, and he was not so weak as to be unwary. Buildings meant danger.

But it was also near buildings that he had found Duchess, and there was the thin calling of remembered things running through him faint and soft as a whisper, so he came a little closer.

A door banging turned him. Startled head held high, he began walking back toward the marsh. Then he heard the dog. No barking, just the air going from its lungs each time its thrusting legs struck the earth. A hard-running dog, breathing in bursts. Duke turned almost as the dog was on him. In a thrust of legs and wings he got into the air, but his wings carried him only a little way, and then the dog was on him.

Instead of fighting back, Duke thrust out his long neck, but the dog's teeth did not close over it. Instead, the dog held the goose to the ground with its front feet and barked frantically.

Duke turned his head. The dog's red, dripping tongue was inches from his eyes. He tried to lift and strike out with his hard bill, but the dog was heavy, and he could not get leverage.

Then a boy came running, and the boy said to the dog: "Okay, Buck." And when the dog got up, the boy bent down, and clasping both arms tightly around the gander and holding the long neck with strong, sure fingers, lifted him from the ground.

Duke was helpless in the boy's grip, because the boy had obviously handled many geese and knew how to immobilize them so they couldn't harm him or themselves.

With the dog jumping alongside for yet another smell of the goose, the boy walked back to the farm buildings. He went to a low shed which held the geese Duke had heard gabbling, and opening the door, went inside. Then he put Duke to the ground carefully, and releasing him in one swift movement, stepped back.

For a moment the gander did not realize he was free. Then, when he knew no one was holding him, he rushed forward with wings flailing. He went straight for the window, but the wire mesh across it threw him back. Stunned, he sat for a moment, and then seeing the boy, he threw himself again where the sunlight came through, and once again he went over backwards, bruised.

The boy quickly stepped out and closed the door, and the gander sat quietly looking at the huge geese he was sharing the building with. They were like no geese he had ever seen. Their rumps touched the ground. They had a comb-like crest on their heads and above their bills. They were so wide and fat and tall they could not walk with the studied stealth of a wild goose, but waddled awkwardly from side to side.

Now that the boy was gone, Duke lifted to his feet. The tame geese moved away from him and gathered in a group to one side of the shed, their bright eyes looking him up and down. Duke went straight for the light of the only window. It was low enough so he could put an eye to it by stretching his neck, but though it admitted filtered rays of the sun, it was nevertheless too grimy to see through. He walked in front of it, back and forth, neck craning to see if here where the light came in there might not also be some way out.

Once the boy opened the door to look in, and Duke stopped pacing to turn and face him. The boy quickly shut the door, and Duke went back to pacing. He walked until evening, and then when a dim bulb near the roof of the shed cast a glow, he came down to crouch on his webs.

Outside there were farm noises of animals being fed, cows being milked. There was the clump of boots and the clatter of pails, and now and then the harsh bark of a dog and the more muted sounds of human voices.

The tame geese clamored, and then the shed door opened abruptly. The boy came in and closed the door behind him. He poured a pail of water into a large, shallow pan, and from another pail he spread corn.

The tame geese clumsily jostled one another for the corn, but Duke stayed on his webs by the window. When the tame geese had fed and drank and plumped themselves to the earthen floor, Duke went over to the feeding spot, but all the corn was gone.

Tilting his head left and right, he looked warily at his strange bedfellows. Then he sipped water, and walking gracefully, went back to his place by the window and settled down as had the rest.

So the place beneath the window became his place, and the next day he paced again as though there might yet be some way out that he had overlooked, but when it was feeding time he moved in among the tame ones to get some corn, but they drove him off, and the first time he walked away because this was their territory and he did not know what feeding rules there were among them.

But the second time the boy brought corn, he was too

hungry to run, and he struck out at a goose, and his thrust, though it was weak, was like a lance compared to their feeble fumbling, and the goose fell back, and the others stood off to watch while he picked up the hard kernels swiftly until his crop was swelling. Then he took a drink and went back to his place.

So the days passed, and outside Duke knew winter was hard on the land, because frost rimed the window and door edges and a snowdrift put a shadow so high on the window he could not lift his head above it. Sometimes the tame geese challenged him, but not often. With the return of strength came the ability to bash the brains from any of the tame ones with a single blow, and a few hard body thrusts had taught those who would question his right to feed and rest here to mind their own business.

Imprisoned as he was, he remembered the winters of his first two years, the ones spent in the south where there were always some greens and acres of fresh water and a whole wide and sometimes wild sky to go riding the wind on.

But so much as the yearning for freedom was a part of him, so also was a wisdom rare in birds, and it was this ability to cope and adapt to whatever life might bring which kept him eating regularly and growing strong of wing.

Any bird or animal of lesser intelligence might have pined away. It happens with species. They lack the ability to tolerate man and aren't capable of relinquishing freedom because their animalistic intelligence quotient isn't high enough to sustain a freedom of spirit while physically confined.

So Duke, though he didn't relish living in the smelly,

close, acrid animal apartment with its one fly-specked bulb, did in spirit surmount his surroundings, and who knows if, perhaps, he didn't live in the greener fields of his dreams?

He must have remembered, else how can a goose come each year directly back to the very hummock upon which it nested the year before? How, in a sky with roadways around the world, can he each year find the right lane back to a precise pothole or an island where corn is spread?

He must have remembered, else why couldn't he forget a mate or four goslings gone down? And if he could remember all these things, how could he ever forget how the sun comes up crimson over a delta to shine on the dew of grass so new it crosses a goose's tongue like velvet?

If he can remember where a river bends, how can he forget blue water and the way it can caress feathers in silvery streams? If he can remember where the gravel bars are and come unerringly, how can he forget the freshness of the wind singing through his feathers as the pack goes barking down the sky in the miracle of migration which is the greatest adventure known to any feathered thing?

So perhaps the memories of these other days sustained him while cooped with such dolts of geese as were good only to stuff with food for fattening. Maybe Duke dreamed of the evening he found the courage to come down from the shining place where he could still see the sun and land in the darkening night behind the wire beside the mate he had chosen.

Perhaps he dreamed of the night when all the world had fallen strangely silent and then on velvet paws the mink had come. The scar from the mink had never feathered over.

When the light was turned on briefly in the evening, it was a bright slash across his cheek.

Perhaps it was because he could remember—which capability is a prerequisite of hope—that he learned to tolerate even the boy, and when he came with the corn stood watching him, but never fleeing again to throw himself against the mesh which covered the window. Perhaps . . . perhaps . . .

But then one day he felt spring. It was in his heart first, and then it came as a tiny trickle of water across his webs as melting snow sent small rivers between the boards to muddy the floor of the shed.

The Canada goose became increasingly nervous, and now he began to pace again where the light was brighter each day as the snow shadow on the window came lower and lower.

All across the country now geese would be moving. From as far away as South America birds would be anticipating the trip back to nesting grounds. A bird's world began and ended with this migration to the place the eggs were laid and the young were born. Everything in between was merely an interlude, a forced time of waiting predicated by seasons so long a part of the world they were ingrained into the fiber of a bird's being.

It was time to go, and Duke knew it. Soon the geese would be back on Heron Marsh, and then after a decent interlude of resting and feeding, they would continue the trip north. Some days, when the wind was right, the gray, paper skies would be penciled from horizon to horizon. He wanted to be among them, with the passing flocks, passing over the checkered farmlands and the smoking cities . . . on and on to where the country flattened out and the rivers ran slowly between low banks and there were great flats of grass and long spits of gravel on which to search for stones.

He wanted to go, but when the time came—if ever— would he be able to? Or would the ghosts of a tragic past try to claim him, and then when the last flock was a faint scribble on a faraway sky, would he have stayed behind? It happens.

THE TAME GEESE with which he shared the shelter were mating, but he watched without interest. Then one day a female without a gander broke away and came over to make herself available. She bowed, and the invitation was plain, but if Duke was interested, there was nothing in his demeanor to show it.

The goose bowed and scraped and chucked deep in her throat and then squatted in front of him. But he only lifted his head higher and walked a few careful steps to one side, and turning his eye, seemed preoccupied with something on the ceiling.

But the big goose was not easily put off. She came again and again to press her suit, until sometimes he was forced into a corner and he could not get away without an indelicate rebuff. She took the pushing, and if she was insulted, she didn't show it.

So now his days became occupied less with dreaming than with avoiding the advances of the overstuffed goose.

Then one night he heard the wild geese calling. The last light had just left the window when the clarion call of a lowering flock came into the building from far out over the marsh where the season's first migrants were letting down.

Usually composed, he forgot himself and ran to the door honking as though they might hear him and come to where he was. Then, when the flock which had landed was silent, he turned and walked sedately back to his place by the window, came up on one leg and cocked his head to a wing.

Throughout the night he came intermittently awake, and freeing his head from his feathers, cocked it first to one side and then the other in a listening attitude. But there was only the wind in the still bare branches of the box elders, and once a small sparrow under the eaves chirped in its sleep, and once the big goose which had been paying him court gabbled excitedly and then stopped gabbling abruptly as though the sound of her own voice had awakened her from a dream.

But in the morning there were more goose packs roaming the sky, and he heard them plainly as some flocks passed directly overhead while touring the countryside looking for a field where the snow had melted and the first green was showing.

Now he strained to his full height to look out the dirty window, hoping to see a gray V cutting across the sky, but the grime of years clouded the pane, yet the gander tried because he was beside himself with the need to fly.

Meanwhile the doting goose pursued him, and he was hard put to elude her as she pressed her suit with ever-increasing fervor. Even at night she left the flock of tame ones to sleep near him, and if he moved a little way toward the door, she got up and moved too.

If he had been a lesser bird, a duck, for instance, he might have graciously and even passionately accepted. Then it would only have been a passing thing of no responsibility, a small affair. But he was a Canada goose, and if the wild ones of the duck world would come even to the city parks to accept the attention of the tame ones which lived there, he could not.

From his enclosure he heard the occasional songbird. There was a first robin cheering just at evening, and now the snowline on the window was gone, and the dirt floor of the pen was sticky with mud, which felt good under his webs.

And, though he didn't know it, the time was for the tame geese to be turned loose, so even like the wild ones they could find their nesting places and start raising families. Already some had started laying, and the boy who had brought the corn picked up the eggs wherever the geese dropped them and carried them away.

Still the goose pursued him, and then one morning when he was straining to hear the honking of a far-off flock and she was pressing toward him, he forgot himself, and turning in an instant of rage, attacked with such fierceness as sent the feathers flying. He drove her all the way across the enclosure, until she was pinned against the wall, before regaining his composure. Then, preening self-consciously, he started to walk away, but before he had half-crossed over the entire flock started after him with a high sound of angry gabbling and much wing beating.

They bore down on him and with force of numbers drove him to the ground and hammered at him with their bills, seeking to beat the brains from his head.

He tried to fight back, but he was so overpowered he could not regain his feet, and he would have died there beneath the beaks and feet and wings and the wrath of the tame ones except at that moment the boy came in and sent the flock scattering.

Duke lay still for a moment and then lifted his head. There was blood on his white scarf, and his feathers were awry, but when he stood, it was squarely strong. He shook like a dog, and most of his feathers fell straight and into place, and those which still stuck out were laid back with his bill.

The boy had left the door open, and the tame geese crossed the slightly raised threshold as quickly as they could lift their rumps. Once outside, they spread their wings and ran flailing the air almost as though they wanted to fly.

Duke, composed now, started to follow the tame ones, but the boy blocked his way. Then the boy backed carefully toward the door, and stepping out, slammed it. Duke was left alone.

He made a careful circuit of the building, as though to make sure none had stayed. Then he went back to his place by the window, and squatting, sat quietly.

Within minutes he heard the boy's boots squishing in the muddy yard. Then the door opened. Once inside, the boy closed the door and then advanced on the Canada goose. In his hand he held a heavy shears.

Duke sat watching, unaware of his intentions to so cut his wings that he would be earthbound as the tame ones, and so unless he walked away, would be forced to spend the spring and summer with the dumpy geese and with the farmyard as his world.

When the boy came too close, Duke opened his wings and prepared to make a run for it. The boy, expert with geese, had anticipated the move and pinned the gander to the mud. Then he wrapped an arm around the gander's body and with fingers of the same hand held his neck.

Once he had the gander immobilized, the boy opened the door and stepped out into the light. The brightness almost blinded Duke after a winter spent in the gloom of the shed. A man Duke had sometimes seen came across the yard from the barn. The boy spoke to the man and then handed him the heavy shears. Then, with his free hand the boy took Duke's right wing and spread the flight feathers until they were a fan in front of him.

The man stepped a little to one side so he could cut down the row of feathers, and the blades of the shears separated and the rasping sound of sliding metal shook the gander, and he felt how loosely he was being held. With a convulsive thrust of wings, neck and legs he was free of the boy's arms and running across the muddy yard, and the black dog came out of nowhere and was pursuing him. But this time he was strong, and his wings lent his feet speed, so before the dog could leap and bring him down, he had lifted and was flying almost blindly and nearly straight up.

On the ground below, the man and boy stood watching, and they marveled, as they watched him go, that a heavy goose could ascend at such a sharp angle into the air.

Duke didn't level off until he was a thousand feet high, and it seemed that it was then he first realized he was free. A wild haronk strained from his throat, and he wheeled on the wind and wheeled again and again until he had circled the farmyard a half-dozen times.

And still the man and boy watched, but the dog had gone back to his dry place on the stoop.

Then the gander went straight in flight until he was only a speck out over the marsh, and the man went back to the barn and the boy went into the house, and the tame geese waddled around importantly inspecting nesting boxes and bowing and scraping and making inane noises one to the other.

Once over the marsh, it was as though the gander remembered the lay of the land, and then he flew south to where two of his goslings had died, and he came low over the field, but he did not land in it. Then he flew east and right through the haze which held Milwaukee and followed the beach north to where the third gosling had been shot. Once again he dropped low but did not land.

Then he turned inland and flew along the route he had taken on the fateful day he had been wounded and came to the exact spot where the fourth gosling had died. From there he flew to the exact center of the refuge, where many geese were gathered, and landed on the water and swam to what was left of the muskrat house on which he had nearly died.

He sipped some water and then climbed to the top of the ragged house and, standing with head high, looked out over the vast land where the first green spears of spring were streaking the dead brown of winter.

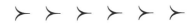

*N*EXT DAY WINTER came back for an encore. During the night the wind had come around to the north, and when the sun came up it wasn't warm enough to cut through the cold, and ice built layer on layer, until the marsh had frozen again and even the rivers were bridged over.

The geese, a wildly winging cloud, lifted with such consternation that the frenzy of it brought villagers and farmers from their beds to windows to watch the mass exodus.

Duke lifted with them to fly south, but after going a little way, he came back and, letting down, skidded along the glaring ice, to come to a thumping halt against a ditch bank.

Again the great marsh seemed deserted. Redwing males, which had come early to stake out nesting territories, had departed with the geese. There were not even any downy woodpeckers rattling away at the dry cattail stalks, nor any chickadees among the island spruce, nor even a crow to fly across the wide loneliness of the empty sky.

Like a ghost goose, Duke wandered from ditch to ditch complaining in low-pitched and sometimes querulous tones, but only the mice heard him, and once a raccoon, which thrust its head out of the hole in a hollow tree, saw him stepping carefully along.

Most of the day he sat on the frozen crown of a muskrat house, his feathers fluffed against the cold, his neck folded back and his bill resting on his breast feathers. But that night, when the moon lifted above the earth's atmosphere, so its red glow changed to a white shine and there was enough light for any goose to fly by, he went aloft and winged north to the Silver Sun Trout Ranch.

A dozen times he circled the frozen ponds and called out, and John Mackenna in his office in the house heard him, and Tom Rank seated in his car preparing to drive home heard him, and the pinioned ones in the shed heard too, and they called back, and Duke cocked his head to their honking, though they had no answer to his query.

In the house Mack turned out the light and lifted a shade, hoping to see Duke's shadow against the moon, and the ranch foreman turned down the window of his car and leaned out. And both men never doubted that it was Duke, though they could not but wonder what brought him back on such a bright night of biting cold.

Finally Mack turned the lights back on, and the foreman rolled up the window, and starting his car, steered it down the drive.

From on high the gander saw the headlights of the car, and, lowering to treetop level, followed on them. Then, when the car turned in at a farm home and the lights were turned off, the gander flew east—straight into the rising moon.

Below, the warmer earth was dimly cloaked in a film of

haze, and when he finally came to Heron, the lights along the shining streets made them look like narrow rivers reflecting moonlight, and he called out as if to see, perhaps, if there were any geese resting there.

And along the streets and in the stores and houses they heard his cry, and it struck a chord in old and young, rich and poor, the hopeful, the despairing . . . though none stopped to think that the heart rending might not be coming from the sky, but out of a well of antiquity within themselves.

And many were envious of the gander's freedom because they were earthbound; and he could travel the roadless wide sky in any direction and to any place. And they never thought how such a routine thing as night makes even a prisoner of the hawk. That life, even for Duke, was a web of restraints. Because how could they know the free flying goose was compelled by some unfathomable urge to fly the night sky, calling out for all such things as should long have been forgotten.

Turning away from Heron Duke flew east and south until he could guide on the moving lights which marked the Madison-Milwaukee highway. He called out when he saw the streaming river of white light, and through an open window a truck driver heard the gander and he relaxed his vise-like grip with which he'd been fighting the wheel all winter knowing that the goose, prophet of spring, called out about balmy nights and sunny days of easy driving.

From city to city he flew, and children jumped from their beds and ran to the windows to look up at the sky. Families came out into the freezing night to stand on the lawn. Shoppers paused, trying to look skyward past the blinding street

94

lights. And who knows what memories and hopes surged in sad and happy procession through these many minds.

In a suburb of Milwaukee a score of school boys leaving a basketball game heard the gander, and the honking sent them scurrying home with visions of wild adventures to take to bed.

Coming to the shores of Lake Michigan, the gander turned north and flew over Mequon, Cedarburg . . . and in a river cottage an old man heard him and put his hand on the head of an old dog; and he remembered the Rock Prairie Days before the geese had been managed and herded so hunters could shoot them like chickens, and when they still came suspiciously to any decoy spread asking among themselves if this was a safe place to alight or should they go graze elsewhere.

And the old man did not feel sorry for the geese, but only for the hunters, because he considered hunting an inheritance graciously made sporting by a code of specific procedures. And he looked to the gun on the peg on the wall remembering a thousand sunrises when its sacrificial boom had echoed in marsh and field and forest, and was sad because there were so few places now where a man might find such solitude as is necessary to practice these rites properly.

Still the gander flew, and it was an incredible phenomenon that this single bird crying out on this moonlit night could be the catalyst impelling so many people to give way to often unsuspected and sometimes long buried emotions.

Some even thought the crying in the sky was the forlorn weeping of a troubled spirit having no haven. Others interpreted it as a challenge. Some thought it sounded like the *stirring bugle calls of their warring days. Others took it as an omen.*

In Sheboygan where the gander flew low, a woman who had forgotten to take in the wash suddenly kicked over the basket of frozen clothes and walked on them until they were soiled with footprints. Then she heard the gander and stood to listen to his promise of warm breezes and, laughing at herself, gathered up the clothes and took them to the basement for another washing.

Turning west at Sheboygan, Duke passed over Plymouth and flew on to cross the shining ice at Lake Winnebago. South a little and he was over Winston, and when he passed over a prison, men went to the windows to stare up at the barred sky hoping for a glimpse of this wild, free flying bird so they might have some symbol of hope to hold to.

DUKE FLEW OVER twenty, thirty, forty . . . villages and cities until the moon was low in the west. Then he came back to Stone River and followed it to where the frozen ditches were a tangle of silver threads and the ponds and puddles shined like the bottoms of overturned tin pails. Here, perhaps lonely and certainly alone, he let down.

*N*EXT DAY, as though aware of an impending weather change, a flock of geese came back to the marsh. They dropped to the frozen river and, ruffling their feathers against the subzero cold, settled down to wait.

Duke had seen them come in, but he did not join them. The restlessness which had sent him winging over central and southern Wisconsin seemed to have subsided. He walked the dikes scavenging for any grass with a tint of green.

Some blackbirds came back. But they were not hilarious, as is their wont in spring, but sat like disconsolate mourners in black.

That night more geese funneled down, and next morning when the sun splashed red the length of the eastern horizon, the blackbirds began to cheer. The warming weather was soft in their feathers.

By noon a rift had opened in the river, and the geese had water. The airways were never empty. By night the geese had turned the ice gray with their groups.

Duke stayed aloof. He made morning flights, a solitary goose, around the perimeter of the marsh and sometimes to greening fields. Occasionally he flew up alongside a formation, and they would make room for him in the spearhead, but he always flew on ahead—alone.

He was strong now, stronger than he had been at any time. He had come to the prime time in a Canada's life, when he should have been guarding a goose, standing sentry for a flock, making decisions about what fields to land on and which to avoid, where to camp for a night.

By nature he was a flocking bird. While the family was being raised and then strengthened to wing, all of his energies should have been concentrated on them. But once the family was strong and sufficient unto any dangers, it was only natural that they join forces with other families to build flocks, which sometimes numbered two hundred or even three hundred birds, and when they took to the air their V spread across acres of sky.

With so many geese, he could not, of course, avoid associating with them. And a flock of fifty invited him to join, and an unattached female of the group detached herself from the main body of geese and swam over to make herself available. But he ignored the other geese and went his solitary way among them.

Each day more geese came. Most flocks winged in high, and then on seeing the marsh with its great concentration of birds, clamored with excitement to be among them. There was always green grass, and it sprouted back even faster than the geese could snip the blades. With such a wealth around them, they could have stayed, but it was traditional of them to nest where the nights were such brief interludes that the sun had hardly set when it was rising again.

This was the enigma of Canadas: Though they might accept the handouts of humans while traveling, there was this need to nest where man's interference was minimal. And though they were capable of adjusting to such inevitabilities as imprisonment, given the chance, they wanted their nests on flatlands far away from prying eyes.

So each warming day the flocks became more anxious to take to the air, bark good-bye, and aiming north, get to the highest place, where the wind could help most, and then, led by some great goose, or occasionally a gander, point the wedge unerringly. Then, if the wind crabbed them off course, they would correct or fly before it until more favorable air currents brought them back. And, if sometimes a storm scattered their flock, mostly they always managed to reform, because after the family, the survival of the community of geese was most vital, and as follows community survival, so the species.

If Duke was infected with the excitement which passed through the great gathering in one tremor of flight after another, he did not show it. He made his way sedately along the ditch banks and floated serenely on the water, seemingly immune to the fever. Any number of unattached females swam hopefully over. But if he saw them, he did not show it. Picking at a tendril or a blade of grass, his eyes seemed always on the horizon. Then, if one or another pressed her suit, he turned on her and drove her back to the flock.

There was always consternation among all the geese when Duke turned on a female. Such behavior they could not understand. It made them swim nervously about, and they uttered sharp little sounds, perhaps of indignation.

But their disapproval apparently did not disturb the gander. If he was embarrassed, it did not show in his demeanor. When a yearning female had been sent packing, Duke always swam back to the rotting island of vegetation where he had almost died, and perched there as though nothing had happened.

So the flocks getting to know him began to avoid him, and it was only when a laggard flock from the south blew in that he was bothered by overtures from either male or female.

Then the last flock arrived from the south, and while they waited, the geese took to touring the countryside, and millions of people thrilled to the sight and the sound of the great gray birds as they flew in strings and wedges from place to place.

And in a few places, though it was illegal, some hid with guns and, shooting quickly, ran out to pick up the dead, and then, hurrying to waiting cars, drove away before the law could zero in on the sound of the shot.

Then, one day, fifteen hundred miles north of where they waited, the ice moved in the flats along the Saskatchewan River. It creaked and groaned and finally broke up in a hundred other streams. The potholes back off from the rivers turned gray with rotting ice and then silver in the sun. From the Pacific Ocean across Canada's provinces and territories to the Atlantic there was a monumental movement.

How the geese on Heron knew is a mystery. But know they did, that now it was safe to fly on, because there would be green grass in abundance by the time they got there. So all day, and on starlighted nights, the flocks lifted, and going higher than they ever did on local flights, pointed north and disappeared.

Several times Duke rose with the departing geese and flew a little way. But always he turned and came back to the marsh.

Gradually the concentration at Heron diminished, until by the time the oak buds had unfurled so their embryonic leaves showed a curl of brightness, Duke swam along the ditches and the river and flew out to the fields, and there were no other geese in the air or on the water or on the land. He was a lone goose amidst thousand of ducks, swirls of redwinged blackbirds, rafts of coots, scatterings of gallinules, spots of rails, chatterings of marsh wrens—biggest bird except for the blue herons returning to their island rookery and once an eagle which flew low en route to a Lake Superior fishing grounds.

Food was so plentiful it took only minutes each day to fill his crop, and he spent the rest of the time like a recluse warming in the sun.

Why had he stayed? Who knows? Except that this was no proper place for a goose now that summer was coming. Was it because here his family had died? But hundreds, thousands of other geese had lost their families, their mates in this self-same place, but they had gone on to the nesting grounds, and most with new mates.

Why had he abrogated flock law? Was it possible that any goose could disobey a law imposed by nature? Was self-determination possible? In a goose? A wild Canada goose?

Decisions based on logic require premises, at least in the human context of thought. But couldn't there be, wasn't there perhaps, something even more profound, something which defies definition in an animal's behavior?

Canada geese are surely swayed by some sort of desires. There is always the choice of this lake or that. This field or the next one. This leader or that guard. They are monogamous perhaps by choice, and after a mate dies, apparently celibate or not, depending on the individual.

So, apparently Duke did have a choice, and his was not to go north, but to stay here on the marsh where his goslings had left him.

Whatever the underlying reason for his decision, he became a surly gander with little patience even for the wrens which flitted about his head, and if, in his meandering, he came upon a nestling duck, he drove the hen into the air, and every time she tried to land to warm her eggs, he flew at her with neck outstretched.

He even chased the muskrats off their feed beds, and swimming a little way, they would lie like chunks of mahogany, eyeing him. He'd swim swiftly after them, whereupon they would dive, and Duke would sit, head high, waiting for them to surface so he could chase them again.

The weather turned sultry. The sun came up red-eyed every morning and sank in a haze of heat each evening. Waters of the ditches and ponds warmed and turned bronze, and fish sought out springholes, and the deer stayed in the brakes belly deep in water. Mosquitoes lifted in clouds to every passing pressure.

Duke watched the west and felt the threat like a fever in the hollow of his bones. It was a thing which can happen in Wisconsin in late May or early June. Suddenly it is summer, brazen and boiling, and the earth has not been made ready for such insistent heat, and elemental forces at odds skirt the edge of upheaval.

Ducks stayed on the water. Redwings left off fighting.

Wrens did not twitter. Hawks stayed in the high trees, because their element, the air, was stagnant.

Even appetites diminished, and a raccoon could be satisfied with a half-dozen crayfish when it usually took two dozen to stay his hunger. Terns flew, but listlessly, not voicing their continual cant. White-throated sparrows tried a few bars and then were abruptly silent. Frogs tried but could not lift the measured beat back to a choir of voices. Duke quit harassing his neighbors.

That evening the sun splashed blood-red on every cloud. The moon was down, and in the night the heat lay with such a weight on Wisconsin, even the crickets were quiet.

Next day the brazen sky never showed the skirt of a cloud until late afternoon, and then over the horizon lifted the first jagged edges of a storm. The one cloud seemed to suck, as though by osmosis, other clouds into the sky, until the west was a mountain range of peaks and canyons and cliffs with the sharp rime of sun rays putting a snowy edge of brilliance to the tumbling tops.

Once above the horizon, the massed winds, marshaling rain and hail, moved swiftly to the drums of thunder.

In the counties of Green Lake, Columbia, Dodge, Dane, Fond du Lac, sharp warnings came through crackling static. Men looked fearfully to the west. Those in cars drove swiftly for shelter. Mothers herded children to basements. Police and fire forces went on alert. Weathermen worried at radar screens. Fishermen retreated to shore. Cattle ran for the shelter of barns. Squealing pigs became ominously silent. Wisconsin waited, but for some storms it knew it could never be ready.

The tornado was born full blown west of the town of Randolph in south-central Wisconsin. It was no ordinary funnel with a little whiplashing tail, but a storm nearly a mile wide with two tiny tornadoes far to the rear and on either side like outriders.

It moved nearly fifty miles an hour, and sympathetic winds whirled with it a hundred miles in every direction. The great funnel arched far forward, so the tail looked as though it was dragging and the vortex was lost twenty-thousand feet high in the clouds.

With a flick of its tail it flattened five farmhouses at the city limits of Randolph and then lifted to spare the city. It touched down again near Beaver Dam, and lifting four trucks, stacked them side by side in a marsh.

It lowered near Quadrangle Inn Corners and, picking up a cow, set her down in a strange pasture where she went on grazing as though nothing had happened.

Then it came to Heron and hovered there, a mile-wide funnel of violence shredding the atmosphere with a whining roar heard for fifty miles. The pressure set up a trembling even in the wells and sewers, and the Stone River below the dam rose three feet into the vacuum it created.

But it did not come down to smite the city, though it sucked the flag from the mast at the post office, lifted twenty roofs and tumbled them into the street, carried a man across the bridge and broke his arm and instilled proper humility into a thousand souls.

Then abruptly the funnel headed north, straight to where Duke sat waiting and watching on the muskrat house. Over the southern half of the marsh it dipped, and Duke and some farmers along the perimeter saw a water spout as the tornado sucked up the sloughs and all their denizens.

Populated with frogs and fish, mallards and a mink, sticks and stones, and one boat and hundreds of other water and shore and song birds, it headed for the federal end of the marsh.

Duke squatted as the forward fury of the winds hit him. There came a rain of fish around him, and he saw the boat come down to bury its bow in a mud bank, so it was standing on end.

Still the gander might have been spared, except that in the instant that the boat crashed down he decided to fly to the thick safety of the rushes. He had only to expose a few inches of wing, and the wind had a grip on him. In seconds he was caught up in the vortex, a helplessness of feathers being lifted higher and higher.

Below, the marsh whirled. Lightning slashed past cleaving clouds. Rain smote the gander, and the transparent film slid down over his eyes to protect them from the onslaught. Edge winds shunted him closer and closer to the center of the funnel. Then an errant whiplash of wind whipped him into the eye of the hurricane-like tornado, and he dropped like a stone. He spread his wings to keep from crashing, but there was not enough substance to this air so the feathers might get a grip. Only a twist of the tornado's tail, saved him from being smashed onto Main Street of Winston. A hundred feet from the ground, the winds wrapped themselves around him, and again he went sailing.

The entire tornado lifted, and the goose was lifted with it. Tom Rank and John Mackenna stood on the porch of the house at Silver Sun Trout Ranch and watched it go over. Debris cluttered the air around them.

Higher and higher the tornado lifted, and Duke went with it. Northward over Oshkosh. Past Appleton. The goose was up to ten thousand and fifteen thousand feet. Rain froze now on his feathers. Twisting. Turning. Sometimes floating placidly. Then the tail of the tornado whipped downward in an arc and cut a half-mile swath through the Nicolet National Forest.

The storm lifted again, and the gander was lofted to eighteen thousand feet, where the temperature was fifteen degrees. Twenty thousand feet, and the air growing thinner.

Then finally the tornado had come so high there was not enough atmosphere to sustain it, and the force was shattered like glass, with winds going off in every direction.

The gander felt himself falling, so he tried to fly, but having gone so long with insufficient oxygen, he lost consciousness. Equilibrium gone, balance went with it, and he turned slowly end over end.

But he hadn't stopped breathing, and at twelve thousand feet his lungs were giving oxygen back to the blood. At eight thousand feet he opened his eyes. At six thousand feet his eyes came into focus. At three thousand feet he tried his wings and managed to divert his fall into a slide. At a thousand feet he brought his big body level, and then the wings began to bite the air. He flew, but with a lurch.

On front winds of the storm he staggered fifty miles in thirty minutes, and then a thousand feet below and a thousand feet ahead he saw through the rain a chain of lakes. Tipping earthward, he began a slant. With a slight stagger at the end of each wing beat he crossed over into Michigan, and then he plowed down onto the lake and swam giddily over into a slough to recover.

It was long dark before he became oriented. The wild ride had so dissociated him from anything earthly that like one who has been drugged he had to let each of his senses slowly find its own way back. When he could comprehend, he discovered he was on crystal-clear water among pencil reeds in a bay hemmed in by a rocky shore. The water was cold. The night was cold. When the sun lifted, the shore grass was slightly frosted.

Soon as he could see, he began to forage, but this was no fertile place such as a goose would ever come to, but a glacial lake of rockbound beauty void of any floating weed beds, and even the shore grass was wiry and unpalatable. He hunted hard but had to be satisfied with a few snails, a couple of caddis-worms and the outer edges of an anemic water lily leaf.

After several hours of searching for food, he ran on the water and took to the air. He lifted at a slant and almost skidded into the treetops. Clear of the trees, he climbed until he could survey this land the storm had taken him to.

It was a forested land of lakes with no farms to break up the woodlands, and what meadows there were grew only sphagnum moss, leatherleaf and wire grass, because the acidity of what little soil the years had laid upon the rocks wouldn't permit such cultures of juicy grasses as might sustain a goose.

Forces put into motion by the storm were still moving north, so he rode the wind, sometimes skittering through the air like a one-lunger airplane with a faltering engine.

Despite his lurching flight, his air speed was a respectable thirty miles an hour, and the wind gave him an added impetus of twenty miles per hour, so his ground speed added up to fifty.

So Michigan's Upper Peninsula slid south beneath him. Nearing Sault Ste. Marie that afternoon, he came to a scattering of farms in the cutover, and lowering, stumbled to an ungainly landing in a field of three-inch oats. After a quick look around, he thrust out his neck, and with mandibles clipping along steadily, he began to fill his crop.

He had almost finished eating when a man came across the field carrying a gun. Duke didn't let him get within range, but with a haronk of rage ran into the wind, and skidding through the air like a kite, managed to get high enough to level off and resume his lurching flight.

Gradually he learned to compensate for the damaged primary feathers on his right wing by holding back a little with the left. Darkness caught him on the edge of Sault Ste. Marie. He let down and landed in the Saint Marys River. It was no place for a goose. Norsemen and Beavers and other aircraft were taxiing across the water to their docks. Barges and their grunting tugs came up from the locks, and the great shadow of their passing sent him swimming head high wildly for shore. On shore, lights and the roar of vehicular traffic sent him swimming back for the middle of the river.

He would have left, but now he felt a fear of flying in the dark. Gradually the river traffic diminished. Lights went out along the shore. The night was given over to the nighthawks and the muffled thunder of their wings. Swimming to a buoy, he maneuvered to the lee of it and spent the rest of the night in comparatively calm water.

In the morning men wondered about the goose which staggered into the air and went north on the wind with lurching flight. Seagulls complained at such an unusual sight as a goose on the Saint Marys River, but Duke couldn't have cared less, because he wanted only to be free of entanglement and off the oily river so he might come to some place of solitude where in time perhaps his right wing would come steady again with new flight feathers and he'd be free of the fear of falling.

For a while he flew over small hills with lakes set like diamonds in their crowns, and then the land flattened, and he looked down on the Precambrian escarpment covered with trees and lakes for endless miles.

He flew until he came to a lake with a large moose meadow at one end. Here he glided down, but the grass was not goose grass, and when he tried to eat, the blades were a cutting sharpness on his tongue and throat.

While he foraged for just one blade of a more velvety texture, a cow moose came out from the fringe of willow, and wading belly-deep into the meadow, put down her elongated muzzle until her mulish ears were all the way under. When she lifted, water drained from her spade face, but between her jaws were lily tubers, and she masticated slowly while eyeing the big goose sitting on the slender cut of water which meandered through the meadow.

Duke watched too while the moose moved slowly along, leaving a muddy trail behind. Then he swam over, and positioning himself in the animal's wake, he began to gobble the insects the moose was churning to the surface. It was no feast. Some of the insects were bitter on his tongue, but he ate indiscriminately, swallowing even bits and pieces of tuber which fell from the moose's jaws.

When the moose had dined, she turned slowly and moved to high ground, where a calf was waiting. She stood then in the shadows of the spruce so the young one might nurse, and Duke went back to the winding cut of clear water and followed it out to the lake.

He had never rested on such clear water. He could see thirty feet to the bottom and watched lake trout chasing minnows, and northern pike coming to the slough to look for young muskrats or any living thing.

By human standards it was a wilderness wonderland of purest water, rocky shores, cat spruce and pungent pines. But for Duke it was a wasteland of infertility, and though he could surely have survived, he would have traded it for any mudflat with short grass and one bar to gravel on.

So he ran on the water and lurched to the air. The wind had lain down, so he circled several times, but then flew north.

He spent two days flying, resting, feeding. An endless procession of clear-water lakes passed beneath. He crossed some wide rivers, including the Albany. He crossed the fifty-first parallel and kept going until he had crossed the fifty-fourth, and beneath him flowed the Winisk River on its way to Hudson Bay. He looked down and knew that this was it—goose country.

*T*HE WINISK, a river of many moods, flows through the land of the Cree and the Ojibwa, through a land of little sticks, that remote northwest corner of Ontario where death waits for mistakes. Here there are trees only along the river. Elsewhere the land succumbs to tundra.

But if it was a place where death bides its time for humans, it was a sanctuary for such a one as Duke. Below the swirling rapids and roaring falls, between the lakes which could be churned to maelstroms of foam, were wide mudflats covered with the velvet green of new grass, and here the Canadas nested.

All the way to the salty bay were gathering places for the geese, and as he flew Duke could hear their quiet gabble, see ganders standing guard near big females already incubating eggs. But if he had any need for their company, he did not show it, and when he landed, it was at the confluence of the Winisk and a tributary, and he let the swift current carry him for a mile, to where it lost its force between wide banks, and then he swam ashore and began to graze. Just before that dim time which is night in the north, he lurched into the air and flew to a bar for gravel. Then he came back to the flat place and at the edge of the water tucked one web up into his feathers and, locking the other leg, leaned a little to rest.

An Indian saw him there the next morning, but geese were not on his agenda. He guided his canoe to where a line throbbed from a willow limb, and pulling on it, flopped a thirty-pound sturgeon to the shore. The Indian tied one end of a rope to the sturgeon, another to a tag-alder bush, and threw the fish back into the water so it would stay alive and fresh until the plane came to make its weekly pickup.

The sturgeon made fast, the Indian shot his canoe against the current and around the bend. Duke turned then to graze where there were other geese on the flat, but he did not go near them, and they showed no interest in his presence.

When his crop was full, he ran into the little wind and faltered aloft. At three hundred feet he leveled off, and after a half-mile he could so compensate for the damaged feathers that the lurch was barely discernible. He made a tour of inspection and found the Indian camp of at least two families on the high ground of a peninsula. He smelled the smoke of their fires.

Circling, he went downstream, and ten miles below, winged over another tent toward which two white men in a boat were towing a log for firewood. Both looked up, and both immediately noticed the lurching flight, though not one in a hundred other humans would have detected that anything was wrong with the gander.

Satisfied, Duke flew back to where he'd spent the night and, lowering to the river, let down. He swam to the bank and lazily began an inspection of the shore. He turned stones, probed the mud, pecked at the bleached branches of a caribou's discarded antlers, sent a school of small brook trout shimmying from a trickling creek down to the river. He ate grass when he found an especially succulent patch, stood eye to eye with a fox until the little animal whimpered and went running. He heard a crashing among the little trees and saw a bull moose with velvet antlers being driven to water by a whirlwind of black flies. He swam out and dipped to run water over his feathers and tried again to preen the broken flight feathers so they'd lie straight.

A week went by, and then the good feeling began to pall and the restlessness was on him, so sometimes he came instantly awake during siestas to look sharply around, and several times in the night he cried out as though tortured by dreams.

During his times aloft he noticed that the two men in the downstream camp were gradually moving south toward the flatland where he headquartered. Then one morning he heard their motor and saw them turn their boat into an inlet across the river. While he watched, they strung a line between two little trees and draped canvas over it.

That afternoon they crossed the river, and Duke left the grass flat to make way for them. They landed the square-stern canoe at precisely the place where Duke had tramped the mud flat and hard. The gander circled once, arching his neck to watch, and then took off downstream to another flatland of short grass.

Toward evening he came back. The men were in camp, and a thread of pale smoke was lifting from their fires and spreading a blue-white haze among the trees. Where he had previously camped he was surprised to see a quantity of corn sharply bright in the slanting sun. He was tempted to lower to it, because he remembered vividly the feasts at Heron and how the corn was a comforting and crop-filling source of such lasting energy as no amount of grass could provide.

But he was wary of such munificence and flew, instead, to the farthest upstream end of the flat and put down there.

The two men watched him, and then, when he had landed, they went back to their supper of brook trout, and one said to the other: "He's a wise one."

When the sun was well up the next morning, Duke flew downstream to see if the corn was still there. No other geese had found it. He came low, looking for a trap. The ground around had been disturbed, and there was a half-moon of what looked like a coontail moss washed up by the river to dry in the sun.

Lifting a little, he flew over the tent, but the men were not there, so he searched the river, and he could not find even their canoe, and it seemed strange they should have left, because their tent was still among the trees, and he could see the shine of some pots and pans.

He came lower, but staying well away from either shore, flew up the middle of the river with eyes prying such hiding places as he remembered hunters had used. When he could find nothing, he lifted again to come over the bait of corn.

Making a wide swing, he came so low his wing tips almost brushed the mud. Then he abruptly lifted to see if his lowering flight had triggered any hiding thing into making an indiscreet move. But there was nothing.

Hungry, he called out sharply. He listened. All he heard was the distant gabbling of a guardian gander, the chucking of a mallard looking in to see if his hen was safely squatted over her eggs, and the splash of a sturgeon caught on an upstream setline.

He came back, and from two hundred feet up spilled air from his wings, to come tumbling straight to the bait. On the ground he stood head high for a full minute, like a stone statue of a Canada goose, never blinking or moving a feather.

Then slowly he turned his head from side to side. When nothing happened, he tilted his head at an angle so an eye was looking directly at the corn. From his throat came a trembling sound so soft the feathers of his neck barely moved.

Once more he lifted his head, and turning it slowly from side to side, looked for danger. Then he lowered his neck and thrust out his head to pick a piece of corn as delicately as a swallow sweeps to sip water. With the corn between his mandibles, he lifted his head, and turning the kernel, tried it on his tongue as if to see if within the very corn itself there might not be some threat. Finally satisfied, he swallowed the corn, and while waiting for it to journey down his long neck to his crop, he looked around.

With the corn a kernel of satisfaction in his crop, he began to feed. When that which he could reach had been eaten, he took a step. The webbing on his right foot came down on a lightly covered trigger set to detonate two small cannon-like devices which had been all but buried in the mud.

The twin explosions set him back on his tail feathers. He saw the net lift, but before he could make a move, it shot up in an arc to come down over him. In spite of every precaution, he had walked into a trap set by men who, during years of study, had come to know the Canada goose better than the Canada goose knows itself.

He was so stunned by the explosion he neither fought the net nor saw the canoe come streaking out of a hiding place where a thrust of red willow and stunted poplar came down to the water. Only when the men were standing over him did he begin to fight back. But he was quickly and humanely subdued, as strong arms and hands closed over his wings and around his legs and long neck.

Most wild ones—even a wolf—on being rendered so completely helpless, would have bowed to the inevitability of death. But not Duke. On being lifted from the net, he was alert for a chance to escape or to stab out at his enemies with his bone-hard bill and to flail at them with the elbow-hard ends of his wings.

But these were no farm boys accustomed to catching fat barnyard geese for the chopping block. These were accomplished biologists adept at trapping everything from moose and bears in great crates down to birds no larger than a man's thumb in wisps of webbing.

While one man held the goose, another took a yellow plastic collar and fastened it to Duke's outstretched neck. They examined his broken flight feathers, took a blood sample into a small syringe, put him in a bag and hung him on a scale for weighing. They took a couple of lice from his breast feathers, fingered the mink scar on his cheek, plucked one tail and one wing feather each, and then while one sat and wrote into a small notebook, the other took the gander to the edge of the water and gently put him down.

Duke could not believe he was free, and he lay on the river's edge, wings outstretched, his feathers wet from the excitement of having been handled. The men backed away, and he watched them. Then he exploded and propelled himself with his wings across the water.

But he did not fly. Instead he spread himself on the river, and lying low, like he might have if hiding, let the current take him, until the two men on the shore were indistinct in the distance. Only then did he lift his head and ride erect on the water.

Two miles downstream he angled toward shore. Coming into calm water, he swam toward an outcropping rock and climbed onto it. Standing above the river, he looked down and saw his reflection—a great gray goose wearing a ridiculous yellow collar.

He moved his head up and down, and the plastic crackled. He tried to curl his neck back in the comfortable fashion which characterizes a contented goose, but he could not. He stood on one leg and with the claw nails of the other web scratched to try to dislodge the neck band.

For the better part of two hours he fought the collar, and then, ruffling his feathers until he was the picture of dejection, walked slowly and complained morosely.

It was two days before Duke would take to the air. By then, if not accustomed to the collar, he was reconciled to wearing it.

In flight the collar was less troublesome than when on the ground because in the air his long neck was always stretched straight out. At an altitude of two hundred feet he followed a dry slough back from the river until he came to a meadow where there was a plentiful scattering of other geese, and then for the first time he noticed that some of these were also wearing collars.

If his neighbors were irritated by the mark by which men followed their flights across the continent, they gave no sign. Then in a puddle Duke also noticed a swimming fuzz of ducklings, and instead of being golden brown, they were vividly pink. He attached no significance to the brood's strange coloration, but was aware only that they were brightly out of harmony with their habitat. The biologists had injected coloring into each egg of a duck's clutch.

If misery loves companions, Duke was an exception, because he took no comfort in the fact that some of the other Canadas were marked. Instead, like a wildling albino sometimes rejects or is rejected by the more normal society of its kind, Duke looked for a place to sulk unseen. He crossed on out of the meadow and flew across one winding slough after another, until he came to a tributary stream of the Winisk, and following it, came to a wide place held in by low rocks into which stone-crushing cold and spring floods had worn crevices and caves.

Here there were no other geese and only a scattering of ducks, because it was not a likely place for waterfowl. There seemed to be food enough, though it was not plentiful, and the rock outcropping was a natural haven for wolves or wolverines, foxes or coyotes—the meat eaters which, though they might hunt the tundra, looked to just such places for dens.

So, while he swam aimlessly about in the middle of the wide place in the stream, two pairs of green-cast eyes watched from a resting rock near the top of a small bluff. The four eyes belonged to two wolves, parents of a litter of five youngsters wrestling at the mouth of a cave a hundred feet from where they lay.

One of the wolves was black. The other, the female, was dark across the back, shading away to almost white undersides. They had just fed on the last of a moose calf, and their interest in the goose was purely academic. Geese did not come to this place, so they were alert only to the fact that the wide pool had something on it which usually wasn't there.

Not that the wolves didn't recognize Duke for what he was—a goose. They had both eaten geese, but it was later in the year, after the birds had been dealt flightless during the molt, and then sometimes in fall when birds wounded by the Indians were discovered hiding where water came into the willow brakes.

Duke drank, and the water had the fresh, flat taste of a stream so young it has not traveled far enough to pick up flavors from roots or rocks. Then he swam opposite a shallow slough and, edging to shore, walked from the water.

The wolves used this flat, but only to move out across the tundra away from their den. Duke could see their trail clearly, but what didn't register with him was how it sharply deviated in one place to bypass an old trap some Indian had long forgotten.

The trap, though weathered and rusty, had never been triggered, and though the man smell had disappeared from it months before, the wolves still avoided it.

Having inspected the dry slough, and satisfied that it had grass to suffice, Duke went back to the water and drifted out to try to compose himself sufficiently to sleep. In the two days since the biologist had demeaned him by affixing the collar, he had hardly slept. Each time he tried to curl his head back to a wing pocket, the plastic crackled and wrinkled, and he came instantly alert.

Gradually, however, the collar had been shaping itself to conform to the fluid contour of his neck. Now warmed by the sun, it had softened, and he put his head back to tuck it beneath a wing. He slept, and when the breeze drifted him toward shore, he swam slowly, only half-awakening, right back out to where he was safe.

When he awakened, the sun was loafing along the horizon. There would be no real night, but since geese are not necessarily monophasic but can, like cats, be polyphasic and indulge in naps, the absence of true night made no noticeable impact on his physiological well-being.

Desiring perhaps to know more about the area he had selected as a retreat, he went aloft and began circling. He discovered the wolf family at once. The dog wolf had just come back from a hunting trip and was regurgitating a partially digested hare, and the young were crowding each other ferociously to get a fair share. Duke was not concerned. The wolves belonged, and ordinary precaution would keep their teeth from his throat.

He saw a moose in the stunted poplar, a pair of ptarmigans, songbirds among the tree leaves and one goldeneye drake resting on the water beneath an eye-like hole in a hollow tree where a hen was obviously warming eggs.

He flew upstream to where the little river gathered its initial strength from a welter of tiny creeks and sloughs. The river's source marked the end of an old and much eroded esker—long sand and gravel ridge left by a river trickling beneath the great glacier.

He followed the esker, traditional migration route of the caribou herds, to where it petered out in muskeg, and then turned back.

Back on the waters of what a biologist might have aptly named the Wolf Widening, he drank and then swam ashore to leisurely graze. Sometimes he almost forgot the collar, and then a quick turn of his head to sharply eye his flank would remind him of it. It was becoming something he might learn to live with, but there wouldn't be a day on which it wouldn't remind him of the hand of the man who put it there.

While he grazed, the elder wolves watched. Ears erect, they lay side by side looking down from their promontory. It was an amusement for them to watch the goose step gracefully along, but they had no designs on the bird.

So the arrangement was idyllic. Duke sensed his haven was remote, else why the wolves? He had water, and the grass of the flatlands was plentiful enough.

Even the wolves welcomed the goose. They couldn't have asked for a better watchdog. Duke's eyes were far-seeing, farther than the wolves'. What's more, he flew a daily patrol, scouting out the country to see if any alien thing had moved in while he slept. And the wolves were tuned to take a warning from any living thing—the jays, a startled ptarmigan, a scurrying hare. . . .

So for Duke there was only the matter of the collar, and it irked him especially when he got a glimpse of his reflection in the crystal-clear waters. And then, of course, there was the trap. But Duke didn't know about this, and it really was no great hazard, because it covered only a few square inches of ground in an area which could be measured by hundreds of square yards. Odds were that no living thing, let alone Duke, would step into it.

So for the gander the days and brief nights passed in a somnolence of eating, drinking, swimming, washing, preening . . . and only rarely did he try to dislodge the collar. The wolf pups grew larger each day and began making exploratory trips down to the water and to the edge of Duke's meadow. The adult wolves had to hunt harder to fill the five expanding bellies, and now they rarely found time to lie and look down on the goose.

Then, though it does not seem possible, Duke began exhibiting a proprietary interest in the wolf pups. Perhaps it was because he could not deny his heritage as a family and a flocking bird and because he recognized the relative helplessness of the youngsters. Tame geese have been known to mother kittens, of if mothering is the wrong word, close association has induced a guardianship complex, and the feathered ones have fought to keep the rest of the flock from killing a kitten.

Whatever—when the pups ventured too far out onto the meadow, Duke reminded them in muted goose language to get back to their cave. The pups, never understanding, were only tempted by the sounds to explore further. Then Duke would haronk with no uncertain sharpness, and the pups would flop back on their haunches, and with ears valiantly trying to stand erect, look with lively interest across the meadow where the goose stood.

Meanwhile the meadow grass kept rising, until it was

almost high enough to tickle an adult wolf's belly, and, of course, it toughened in the process. So Duke took to following the wolves' trail, because along its edges there were always new sprouts, and these his tongue could relish, so there was always a sufficient wetness in his throat to slide them easily to his crop.

Many times the gander took the little detour around the trap which was completely camouflaged by grass. Then one day when he was coming down the trail busily searching out the youngest tendrils, he heard a distant drone. But airplanes being no new thing, he did not at first look up to see from where or which way the big bird was flying.

It was only when the Norseman bore right down on the wolves' promontory that he looked up. The plane came so low that prop wash flattened the grass, and the engine roar was so loud Duke felt his feathers involuntarily flatten against the danger of the sound.

It was the fish plane come to pick up sturgeon along the river and en route to check out likely places for wolf packs so government trappers might put out poison baits before the caribou came.

Duke was sure the big bird was aimed to pounce on him. After his initial freeze at the fright of it, he ran down the wolf trail to get into the air, where he would be on more even terms with his adversary. And he might have made it, but where the wolf trail made the dogleg turn to go around the trap, Duke went straight ahead and then—snap—and the rusty jaws closed over two toes, and he was caught.

His momentum carried him, trap and the rotting log toggle to which it was wired, off the ground, but he could not sustain the effort, and the great weight brought him crashing back.

The pilot, all unaware of the gander's predicament and satisfied only that there were wolf pups among the rocks, lifted the plane a few hundred feet and headed for the big river.

Duke sat trembling, and then he panicked. Thrashing the air with his wide wings, he dragged the trap and toggle across the meadow dangerously close to the wolves' den.

The pups, on hearing the commotion, came to the edge of the flat ground, and sitting in a row, watched. The goose was unaware of the wolves. He fought the trap with all his strength until slime ran on his breast feathers and his beak was agape as he gasped for air.

Gradually, then, the fight went out of the gander, and when it did, the pups dared to come closer. Duke saw them, and if he'd once felt inclined to be fatherly, now every vestige of kinship was gone and they were the enemy. He thrust out his neck and hissed, because he knew if the old wolves came back he would surely die.

When the pups made no move to come closer, Duke once again beat furiously with his wings and again managed to drag the chain and toggle into the air. But he could not sustain the effort and tumbled back in a disarray of feathers.

Then he lay there, his wings spread wide and his head and neck undulating as though unwilling to give up, but not having the strength to continue the struggle.

One of the pups got up and advanced toward him. When it was within a few feet of the prostrate goose it stopped to sit back and cautiously survey the trapped gander. Duke hissed, but the pup disregarded the warning, and getting up, advanced to where it could get a wing tip between its teeth and start pulling.

Encouraged, the four other pups ran down to rally around the biggest and bravest of the litter. One playfully nipped at the goose's tail feathers, while a third went around for a muzzleful of feathers on the other wing.

Duke struck out with his wings, and all the pups went tumbling backward. They retreated a little way and waited until the gander stopped struggling. Then with little growls and snarls and anxious whimpers they rushed in again. The goose met their advance with a thrust of wings. Again the attack was repulsed. But now it was a game, and instantly the goose was quiet, they came charging in.

In an attempt to keep his flight feathers from being destroyed, Duke tucked in his wings. The bravest of the young wolves sprang for his neck and would have gotten his needle-sharp teeth perhaps in the jugular except for the plastic collar. The pup's teeth went through the collar, and he closed his jaws and began to savagely shake his head.

Another pup closed in on the other side. He too went for the gander's neck and got a mouthful of plastic. With a wolf pup on either side, the gander was yanked about, the fulcrum in a tug of war.

Duke's neck might easily have been broken, except that the plastic, warmed by the sun and the goose's overheated body, expanded, and when the gander reared back, his head slid out of the noose.

Unaware, or not caring that the goose had escaped, the pair of wolf pups went on with their tug-of-war. Snarling and growling, they braced with necks outstretched as each tried to wrest the piece of plastic from the other.

During the momentary respite, Duke put up his head to see both adult wolves standing at the den site looking down on the wild antics of their litter. He looked behind, where the other three pups were generating enough courage to attack.

Then, as the adult wolves started down to put an end to the goose, Duke made his last effort to get into the air. Unable, with the trap clamped to one web, to run, he had to lift himself with wing tips braced to the earth. He made a mighty effort and lifted, and the rotting toggle broke where the wire had cut into the wood, and he was in the air with the chain and the wire dangling beneath.

But the weight of the chain and the trap kept him from ascending, and he could only maintain his position a few feet above the ground. One of the pups, fascinated by the swinging chain, ran and made a dive for it. He got it between his jaws, and for the fraction of a second the wolf pup was suspended in air like a furry pendulum. Then the added weight of the pup was enough so the jaws of the trap slipped free of the gander's toes. The pup fell back with the trap on top of him, and Duke went off at a wild, winging slant for open water.

The gander, though his foot was not seriously hurt, was in a state of shock when he hit the water of the Wolf Widening. Only feather ends quivered when, led by the adults, the excited litter of pups ran to the water's edge. Immediately the biggest and bravest pup went beyond its depth and began swimming. Shocked by the chilling river, the pup swam with forepaws high, flailing the water. The she-wolf walked out, and grabbing him by the scruff, carried him back, and then with a nip in the flank sent the pup scurrying toward the den.

The adult wolves stood belly-deep to watch. Duke never knew they were contemplating swimming out to retrieve him. The world around—trees and water and grass and sky—was shrouded by the haze of unconsciousness, and he paddled so feebly the effort was only enough to maintain his position in the slight current.

It was the dog wolf who finally launched himself and started swimming toward the gander. At first the wolf swam badly, with his hindquarters dragging. Then the hot scent of the exhausted goose, spreading like an invisible film across the water's surface, touched the wet nerve endings on the black animal's nose, and he thrust powerfully forward, until his back came clear of the water and his bushy tail lifted, until he was brandishing it.

On the shore the youngsters waded out until they were standing alongside their mother, and the punished pup came belly-crawling down the slope to witness the kill.

It was the goldeneye drake, on the water beneath the hollow-tree apartment, who saved the gander. Thinking the wolf had designs on him, the goldeneye turned his gaudy purple head with the white cheek patches for a quick look to see that the hen hadn't come out, and then with a guttural quack of warning the duck ran along the surface and into the air.

The warning went deep past the film of unconsciousness and stirred in Duke an automatic reflex to respond. He lifted his head, saw the wolf's white teeth and the lolling red tongue, and then he began frantically beating the water with his wings and scooted downstream. The wolf knew at once it had been bested, and turning, swam slowly back to shore.

*D*UKE REVIVED QUICKLY. Despite the pummeling the pups had given him, there was no serious wing damage, and when the deadening lethargy of fatigue began to dissipate, he felt only pain where the trap jaws had gripped two toes. Fully alert again, he drank to replenish fluid and then took to the air.

The wolf pack was resting. They looked up when his shadow came across their rocks, and the pups whimpered because it was the closest they had yet been to making a kill. But the adult wolves, red tongues hanging, seemed to be giving him a grin.

However, it was no minor episode in the gander's life, but rather a dreadfully close brush with death, an almost traumatic experience, and he knew he would never come back to the Wolf Widening.

Swinging north, he flew until he was over the Winisk River. Another family had come to the Indian camp, and the pair of biologists still had their tent cross stream from where they had put the collar on Duke. They were in a boat coming upstream when Duke flew over, and of course they recognized him because of his awkward manner of flying, and they were amazed because he wore no collar.

Had they known about the wolves, it would have made

one of the most interesting paragraphs in the paper they planned on preparing, and biologists across the country and from other lands would have sent letters to ask if they were writing fiction or "is this a fact?"

Duke flew with the river, going all the way to the tidal flats of Hudson Bay. Here he rested through a rainstorm, listening to the restless gabbling of yearling blue- and snow-goose flocks as the birds incessantly traded grazing places. Here, before many weeks would pass, tens of thousands of geese from the eastern arctic and subarctic would colonize to wait for a north wind to ice their tails and send them south.

It was a staging area, and already the nonbreeders had come, and these ebbed and flowed in endless procession with the tide. It was an unsettling place for a mature Canada gander, and the old restlessness came over him, until one night when the sun had gone for its brief nap below the horizon, he climbed on a brisk north wind and headed south.

Quickly he was beyond goose country and back over the clear-water lakes of the Precambrian shield. At once the airplane traffic increased, and below, boatloads of fishermen spearheaded white wakes from one fishing reef to another.

He flew great distances despite the damaged wing, and in six days of flying and resting and feeding had reentered the United States, crossed Michigan's Upper Peninsula and come back to Wisconsin.

He went straight to the Silver Sun Trout Ranch and without any preliminaries dumped down on the farthest pond, and hardly had he preened himself than Tom Rank was on the shore with a pail of corn.

John Mackenna came out too, and together the men stood at a respectable distance so the gander could feed.

"He looks rough," Rank said.

"Yes, and he's still a loner," John replied.

"Wonder what happened?" Rank mused.

"Storm, maybe. Could be he got caught in the Big Tornado," Mackenna guessed.

The two men were silent. They were thinking of how the storm had taken such a toll of human life that no one bothered to estimate how many thousands or tens of thousands of birds might have been killed by it.

When they came to where the walk divided into two walks, one leading to the hatchery and the other to the house, both men stopped.

"Likely he's a confirmed widower now," Mackenna said.

Rank smiled. "Who knows?"

They both laughed and went their separate ways, and Duke got up and flew to the river. He rested until evening and then came back for more corn, and now that night was really a time of darkness instead of an interim of half-light, he made the adjustment by staying on the muskrat house.

The gander alternately rested and fed for three days and then headed south again. Over Heron Marsh he first flew to where each of his daughters had died and then came back to the moldering muskrat house where he had almost died.

Food was plentiful in the marsh. And so summer might have passed without further incident, except that one brilliant morning Duke found another goose.

He had taken to the air shortly after sunrise to fly the perimeter of the marsh. Then, instead of coming back, he followed the river south. He went all the way along the shallow valley which holds the Stone River, to where it suddenly bulges out into Lake Bluestone. He was flying low across the lake when he heard a haronk. He scrambled for altitude to get a better look around and spotted the goose to the far north side back in Pluckhan's Bay.

He flew over, circled the lone goose several times, and then glided toward the water, to come to a skimming stop. He swam over to where the goose floated in the middle of a pothole and when he was a few feet from her stopped to look her over.

The female bobbed and made soft sounds of joy at having been discovered by one of her kind. She had been alone since the great mass of geese had continued their journey north. Victim of a gunner come to illegally kill, she had taken several pellets, and now the tip of one wing from the first joint curved back on itself. The wound had healed so that she would be crippled until she died, and there was no possibility that she would ever fly again.

Duke made no advances, but neither did he leave. They swam together until dusk, and then Duke lifted and called to the female to follow. She ran on the water but could not rise. When she did not come, Duke went back and landed on the water beside her.

He swam in circles around her, and then took to the air again. Once more the crippled goose tried to fly. When she could not lift, Duke went for altitude and headed back for the marsh.

He spent the night on the old muskrat house, but in the morning he headed back for the lake. He followed an overland route instead of flying along the winding river, and immediately upon lifting over a wooded hill saw the goose in the center of a pothole below.

He let down beside her, and they spent the day swimming and feeding together, but when night came, Duke went back to the marsh. Seven times Duke made the trip back and forth, spending each day with the goose, but he never offered her any greens. He made no advances.

On the morning of the eighth day they swam out of the pothole into the slough, and from the slough they drifted out onto the lake. The water lay smooth as a sheet of cellophane, and he took her to a weed bed he had sighted from the air and they dined on the tender ends of emerging vegetation.

But if it was the gander's intention to claim her, he made no move to do so. And if she was mystified by his strange behavior, perhaps she felt that it was because the time for mating had passed, and perhaps, if they stayed together, he would ask her in spring.

It was no pressing thing now that summer warmed their backs and the tendrils were so tender they went down without scratching. They had almost filled their crops when Duke first heard the ominous growl of an approaching motor. He swam from the weed bed, and lifting his head, turned it from side to side to locate the danger. She swam behind him, indifferent to the disturbance.

The boat came out of the mouth of the river, leaving a white wake that curled away on either side in a foam of bubbles. Duke uttered a warning and began swimming swiftly for the slough. Alerted now, the goose hurried along behind him.

But long before they got to the slough, the boat's bow was pointed straight at them, and Duke ran on the water to get into the air. The goose ran too, but she could not lift, and when the boat was about to crash over her, she swung hard to the left and it went by.

The goose redoubled her efforts to gain the protection of the reeds, but the boat, swinging a wide circle, came back. Duke started toward the marsh but then turned, and flying above the boat, clamored loudly. It was a strange maneuver for a wild gander, since he had not mated with the goose. It would have been less strange if Duke had had young on the water. In that event, he might conceivably have attacked.

The crippled goose walked high on the water, her wings flailing to give her speed, and again she was just barely able, at the last moment, to swing left with a hard push from her one good wing, to get out of the way of the boat.

Duke sounded in a rage. He bent his head down and hissed. But he stayed a safe distance in the air, and the two men in the boat waved at him as though they were enjoying some kind of game.

By the time the boat had skidded around to make another run, the goose was at the edge of the marsh. She swam swiftly among the reeds, where the boat couldn't follow, and disappeared. From the air Duke could see her follow the dim muskrat trails deeper and deeper into the slough.

Twice the boat circled, and then giving up the chase, turned and headed back toward the mouth of the river.

When the roar of the boat motor had faded, Duke came

down beside the goose, and while she slept from exhaustion, he remained alert and on guard. That day, instead of swimming where he wanted with no concern for her, he kept a sharp lookout and only fed when she was full and could guard.

So it was that he accepted minimum responsibilities of the Canada-goose society. But it was no more than that. He did not search out tender grasses for her, nor touch her with his bill, nor try to herd her before him—but only stood guard.

But he stayed that night and the next, and on the third day, when he would have flown back to the marsh, it was to discover that the molt had dealt him flightless. Resigned to weeks of virtual imprisonment, he spent hours spreading oil from the sac at his tail to his feathers, since he could not go aloft to dry them out. They made a partially submerged log their headquarters, and when not floating and feeding, they stood there with webs in the water.

So the summer passed, and they were rarely disturbed except by the occasional fisherman. Then one September day they saw the first flock of returning geese, and Duke, remembering the corn on the marsh, meant to return. When he took to the air it was with a sure and certain beat of powerful new feathers. Only once the goose tried to follow, and then, as though remembering, she only watched. When she would not follow into the air, Duke came back. Then he swam across the lake with her in tow and started into the mouth of the river.

He swam all day and most of the night against the current. They went past the Rousteau club grounds and there were only a few lights in the cottages. At Log Bridge they heard a car roar above them, and they hurried. Then, when they came to the sloughs above the bridge they rested.

More goose flocks appeared in the sky, and after they had eaten, Duke went back out into the current, and so they came to a small bay below the city of Heron, and here Duke waited for dark. That night he followed the river into the city and swam between the homes, past the church, along where a park came down to the shore . . . until they came to the dam.

They rested below the dam in the darkness until the sounds of the city dimmed, and then while the people slept, they came up on the green bank, walked across the concrete road and down the other side. They swam past a factory, and by the time the city awakened next morning, they were a mile up the river and into the marsh.

Geese were everywhere in the sky at dawn. But they rested and fed in a slough before swimming to the north end of the marsh, where the greatest concentration of honkers and the corn would be.

The corn was a treat after a summer of eating mostly vegetation. They never strayed far from the feeding grounds, and each day they could feel fat coating over their muscles and adding to their reserves of strength. A reserve, had they known it, which would be depleted quickly once the ice came.

And every day and most nights geese continued to trickle in from the north. They came in family groups and some large flocks, and always tired from crossing half a continent. The concentration built steadily from several thousand to twenty thousand and then fifty and then, once again, there were more than a hundred thousand geese on the marsh.

Then inevitably the hunters came. Geese died by the thousands. But Duke made no attempt to leave the marsh even when the daily ration of corn was cut off. Instead, he led the crippled goose back to where springs promoted an extra growth of grass, and though they often went hungry, they did not starve.

Then, quite as abruptly as the shooting had started, it stopped. The government had decreed that Wisconsin hunters had taken their quota of Canadas. There had to be some left for those waiting in southern Illinois, Kentucky, Tennessee . . . all the way south to Louisiana and even Florida.

Once the shooting stopped, the trucks came out with corn, and Duke led the crippled goose to the feeding islands. They lived in luxury. There was always corn. There was enough grass to supplement the fatty ration. There were always little stones for their gizzards. And there was enough water for a million geese.

Nevertheless Duke was restless. Stirring within him was the memory of another autumn when he had been unable to flee before the ice of winter trapped him. Somewhere in the back of his little brain were snowstorms, days without food or water. He could remember how the last of the flocks had left. How the current had finally frozen. How he had wandered across the hard shield of ice weak and sick.

Sometimes now when a flock lifted to go south, he flew a little way with them before turning back to land beside the crippled one.

He never urged her to fly now. He had called from the air so many times without avail, that now he called no longer.

But the mild autumnal weather held the land well beyond

the time for winter. And always there was corn, plenty of corn.

Then surely as ice comes to Wisconsin, the geese began to leave in numbers. But it was no mass migration as in some years, but a gradual movement of families, with only a few large flocks lifting to get into formation. A dozen times Duke lifted with a flock that was leaving, only to come back again.

Then came a night of sharp cold, and in the morning some of the ditches had a skim of ice and some of the potholes were shiny hard. Then for the first time in many weeks, Duke tried to get the crippled one into the air, but she would not even try her wings, because she had become convinced through endless failure that she was flightless.

Finally Duke settled down beside her, and then he folded in his neck until his bill was resting almost on his breast. It could have been described by human standards as an attitude of concentration. But, who knows. Perhaps the gander felt only defeat. Or perhaps he felt nothing of significance, and was only resting because he had tried so hard to get the goose into the air.

That night it snowed, a soft fall of big flakes, and in the morning the cuts of open water were bleakly black in the otherwise stainless white surroundings.

After the pair had fed on the corn, Duke led the goose across the frozen ditch, along a dike, across some frozen potholes until he came to the river.

The air above was speckled with departing geese jockeying to get into flight formation when Duke slipped into the water. When the goose followed, the gander turned north and swam against the current. He stayed near the shore, where the water was not swift, and by swimming all day the pair came by nightfall to the northernmost boundaries of the marsh.

Here, on a frozen hummock of rushes, they spent the night. By morning the frozen edge of the river had widened on each side and the only open cut was where the current ran swiftly. But Duke breasted the current. The goose followed. Behind them the marsh went solidly under ice. They didn't look back. Their way was north.

*N*ORTHERN LIGHTS built icy colonnades in the sky, and then cresting, spilled color—only to gather at the horizon and build again, marble shaft on marble shaft. Beneath the panoramic display the geese rested, and a muskrat came across the snow-covered ice from the open river to peer at them curiously, and a great horned owl on velvet wings lowered, but discreetly decided to forego the pleasure of a goose dinner.

From time to time Duke came awake. The stars, like his eyes, surveyed their surroundings. Then, chucking so far down in his throat it was less than the sound of grass, blade against blade, he turned his head and, tucking his bill into a feather nest, went back to sleep.

They were a splendid pair, each cocked on one leg on the white hummock: big birds with feathers so neatly and firmly interlocked they looked like armored geese impervious to tooth or talon, wind or snow.

But it was an illusion, because they could shiver like any other creature when fuel for their furnaces ran low, when they had to go without food.

But this night they were warm. The feeding stood them in good stead now, and even next morning when a sunrise ran rampant and it seemed the horizon had caught fire, though they were hungry, it was no pressing hunger of great need.

But there was nothing here for them to eat, so Duke walked across the ice-covered snow to the open cut of water, and the goose followed. Then, swimming, the gander headed north through flat marsh country, with scatterings of tamaracks looking dead in their winter nakedness.

He swam steadily and strongly at a speed of more than a mile an hour, and by noon they had come a half-dozen miles and the marsh was so far behind they could not see the crests of the trees which stood in groves on the islands.

The going was slow, but not necessarily difficult. The current was only so strong as to keep the middle of the river open, and the water was warmer on their webs than the air. The sun shone too, and the world was bright and white around them, and sometimes they paused where a turn in the river left a comparative calm, and then they dunked their heads and necks, so the water ran in rivers down their gray backs to go scattering in bright beads across the ice.

But now the need for food was being felt, and Duke swam head high looking left and right for any green morsel. At an abrupt turn in the river, they came upon a surprising lode. Just upstream from the turn in the river, muskrats had been working all night to fill their stomachs. Fragments of vegetation spilling from their jaws floated on the current, to come up against the ice edge at the turn and hang there. There was enough for both, and some left over.

So Duke decided to camp there. They stayed the afternoon and the night, and sometimes they cavorted in the current, and when morning came there were even more green morsels, and having filled their crops, they bobbed on end to search the shallowest places, where they could reach the river bottom to collect a few stones for their gizzards.

But next morning there were no greens because the muskrats had finished with the weed bed and moved downstream.

So Duke began the trek north again—under highway bridges, beneath railroad trestles, past farmhomes, through narrow cuts guarded by high hills, between bone-bare trees of woodlots, down the stretches of flat marshes . . . and always the stream grew smaller and the cut of open water narrowed.

They lived on greens left floating by the muskrats, and though they never found such a lode as had detained them at the sharp turn of the river, they were able to pick up a living as they swam.

Then finally, as had to happen, they came to the end of open water, and stretching before them was a snaking, narrow ribbon of ice. The river had dwindled to a tiny creek, and here, where the current was less than the breath of a bird, it could not stay the ice.

Duke was reluctant to leave the open water. He walked a little way on the ice, and the goose followed, but then he went back. They sat together on the ice edge, and sometimes they made tracks to the banks and dug down with their bills through the light covering of snow to see if there might not be some green thing to fill the emptiness they felt.

Next morning Duke swam back downstream, but then, as though he had made a decision, he turned abruptly, and on coming to the ice edge, gave himself a boost with his wings to get out of the water and started north along the frozen creek.

Together they followed it into a dense little woodlot of small straight poplars, and here, in a marsh pocket, the stream ended. They left the ice and walked through the woods, bearing north and turning only sometimes for a weed seed.

The snow was soft and not uncomfortable beneath their webs. They had no trouble moving at least as fast as they had been able to swim against the river current.

On a knoll they broke out of the trees, and before them sprawled farm buildings. Duke stopped, every nerve tingling, and his feathers lifted to the feel of fear. Then he turned and walked a little way back among the trees. Beneath an oak he began probing and found an acorn.

He did not offer it to the goose as he might have if they had been a mated pair, but swallowed it himself, and then, using his bill like a miniature snow plow, uncovered another. He looked over at the goose, but instead of picking it up and laying it at her feet, he only backed away so she could walk over and eat it.

Then both the Canadas began looking for acorns. They cruised back and forth with their bills plowing along the ground, nibbling a little to sensitize their ability to feel, and by the time they had trampled and probed every inch of ground beneath the tree, each had a marble-filled sack for a crop. Then they ate snow, and when dusk came the goose would have settled next to the trunk of the tree for the night.

But the gander could find no comfort here. It was such an alien place for a Canada goose that he started with even every mouse sound. It was one thing to be forced to hide here during daylight hours, and still another to voluntarily stay when darkness gave them cover under which to leave undetected.

But the goose was reluctant to go. She too found the place not to her liking, but her crop was full, her webs were sore from the ice and snow, and wary though she was of the suffocating closeness of the trees, sleep seemed more desirable.

Still the gander did not drive her. He only walked a little way and waited, and when she did not come, he walked a little farther, and then when he was almost out of sight in the gloom, she got to her feet and followed.

They went across a plowed field downwind of the farmhouse. It is difficult to determine whether Duke stayed downwind on purpose, but maybe he remembered the dog, and he had no desire to make the acquaintance of another.

There were lights in the farmhouse windows, and the geese, with their spectacular eyesight, could see shadows moving across each lighted place, so they hurried until the little rise on which the buildings stood became a vague shape in the background and then disappeared.

They walked all night over such a variety of terrain that by the time the east began to hint at another day, they were exhausted. The goose lagged often, and Duke had to pause for her to catch up.

That day they rested in a small marsh of low grass, and they did not risk putting up their heads lest a man or some other passing predator see the pair of geese in such a vulnerable and precarious place.

When night came they were hungry, but there was only snow, so they ate some, and it revived them enough to continue.

At dawn, bedraggled and swiftly weakening, they stumbled onto a tiny spring which trickled out of a grove of young poplars, and it was like finding an oasis in a world of frightening obstacles. The goose, beside herself at the sight of water, forgot their bond of silence and honked excitedly as she threw herself into the trickle of water which was hardly larger around than her own neck.

While she lay stretched full length letting the water trickle over her tongue and down her throat, Duke, though as thirsty and hungry as he was, stood rigidly erect and on guard. Then when the goose had had enough, he went to the water, but he did not throw himself down, but skimmed it with dignity.

Both drank again and again, and then began eating the green moss from the white stones, snipping the few grass blades which had kept green by the comparatively warm spring water. They didn't rest until noon. By then there wasn't a spear of green left around the small pocket of bubbling water, and they had even dug down a little ways to get the grass roots.

It had been no banquet, but it had been something, and though Duke tried to remain alert and on guard, he caught himself sleeping often during the afternoon.

That night the goose was reluctant to move. If she had been human, she might have argued: "At least we've got water!"

But something was driving Duke. He walked away a half-dozen times before she finally got off her webs to follow. Then they moved slowly. The fat they had hoarded while eating corn on the marsh had all been absorbed by their strenuous efforts.

Still they moved, and always on the North Star, toward where the northern lights sometimes played—through lands which were becoming increasingly more rugged.

It was midnight and a thin slice of moon had just come out from under the clouds when Duke detected the creeping shadow of a fox, and in the same instant smelled the rank odor of the prowler.

With a low, sharp warning he prepared the goose and then swung to face the fox, his head down and wings spread slightly. But the fox was no fool, and it moved quietly just beyond the range of the gander's hard beak, looking for a way to break down Duke's defenses and get a throat hold.

He circled at a safe distance, and Duke turned with the fox. Seeing no way to break through, the animal decided to concentrate on the goose. She stood head high and made no move to defend herself. But Duke walked between the fox and the goose, so again there was no way except to chance the hard beak, the flailing wings.

Around and around they went, the fox, colored like an autumn leaf, with its ears laid back, stepping carefully. The goose, turning like a mechanical goose, sometimes hissing. A weird dance of death, but beautiful. Two superb antagonists. Fencing for a weakness, one in the other. Each seeking survival.

The fox broke first, with a sharp little whimper of impatience. Duke spread his wings a little wider. Then the fox attacked, trying to break past the gander's defenses. Duke's neck coiled and then shot forward. He hit hard with his beak, and then the bony wings began flailing the fox's body. He must have at once cracked a rib, or several. The fox went backward in its tracks, and Duke, sensing an advantage, pressed the attack. The fox fled.

Duke turned to see if the goose was all right. Then he walked sedately back to her, and after preening what feathers had gone awry, he started the northward march again.

The goose faltered often now. Sometimes she went down on her webs and refused to move. Duke halted his march to let her recover.

That morning there was no water. Nor was there any food. They camped for the day in a hedgerow flanked by fields. It was a most precarious place, but it was there that daylight had caught them.

There were cardinals in the hedgerow, and there were nuthatches and chickadees, and in the fields on both sides flits of juncos seeking weed seeds kept up a constant twitter. Some of the songbirds came close to stare with bright little eyes at the strange pair squatting among the brambles beneath the black-cherry trees. Duke did not welcome their attention. Any predator passing might wonder at what the little birds had found and come to see for themselves.

Hunger was now constant. A hundred times the goose and the gander probed the snow in front of where each squatted, as though by some miracle they had overlooked a morsel to give to their crops. But there was nothing, and they had to be satisfied to eat snow, which instead of providing the relief they sought, now began to burn their tongues and their throats as though it were hot instead of cold.

That night the goose moved so slowly the gander had to

stop every few minutes for her to catch up. They searched a woodlot for acorns, but squirrels had cleaned it out. Coming out from among the trees, they saw ahead what seemed like an endless brown sea of grass high above the snow. Walking through woods was difficult enough, but this dense stand of grass was like an impenetrable wall to the faltering Canadas.

Down to the grass, and the goose refused to broach it. The gander walked in, and the grass, which was saw-edged and tough, was higher than his head. He tried for almost two hours to entice the goose to follow. But now she sat as though at last she had come to the place where she had decided to die.

So Duke rested with her, and then, when he had recuperated, ran into the wind and took to the air. The goose called out for him to come back so she would not have to die alone, but he made a circle and then flew north. Hardly had he gained altitude and straightened out his flight pattern when a gleam caught his eye.

He arrowed toward it, and then landed on a large river which had only narrow ice ledges jutting out from either side. After drinking, he ran on the water to get back into the air and came back to where the goose sat. She honked her joy at seeing his shadow against the stars. He landed beside her, and then walked along the fringe of the marsh, and now the goose, fearful lest he fly again, followed.

With the goose lagging and resting often it took most of the night to get around the grass barrier, and it was breaking day before they came to the river bank. The goose was too exhausted even then to hurry, but Duke moved on ahead out across the ice shelf and into the water. Then the goose joined him, and they let the current take them while they drank and ran the refreshing water over their bodies.

Then they preened, not out of vanity, but because with every feather in its proper place they were perfectly insulated against the cold, and what was more important, they were waterproof.

Now Duke started north again, swimming close to the shore where they were somewhat camouflaged and where the current could not get a straightaway cut at their progress as it might in the middle. At intervals, where the ice ledge had lost its grip on the bank and cracked away into the water, they probed the muddy shore for old grass, snails, caddisworms among the stones, occasionally earthworms, sometimes a stray stand of coontail, young reeds tender enough yet to bend between their beaks—odd fare, but if not sustaining, at least a deterrent to starvation.

Shortly after noon they came to where they could see smoke rising from the stacks of a factory and the rooftops of a town. Duke swam them into the mouth of a tiny creek, and between its banks they sat on an icy ledge, and almost at once the goose slept.

The nearness of the town bothered Duke, and he tried to stay awake, but he slept anyway, because the forced march was beginning to take its toll. And each time he slept, his head drooped lower and lower until his bill came to the ice, and that would awaken him and he would come alertly erect to turn his head from side to side, looking for whatever danger might have crept up while his eyes were closed.

But the day passed without incident, and then they started the slow swim north again, and when they came to the limits of the city, they stayed in the shadows of the bank in the hope they might go undetected to the northern limits.

In the center of the city they swam into a maelstrom of water. It was a dam festooned with great overhangs of ice, and the water came crashing to the river to boil away in eddies of foam. Duke swam to the edge of the rough water, and then turning away, went to the bank. Together the Canadas clambered up the steep shore and then walked up and around the dam to where there was a half-moon of open water at the edge of a lake of ice which extended beyond their nighttime vision.

They let down into the open water, and Duke, nervous because of the press of houses around him, hurried across to hop out on the ice and start walking across the frozen lake.

Next morning, people using the bridge which spanned the river above the dam were surprised to see goose tracks. They stared out across the frozen lake, wondering how it could be that in the dead of winter geese had come to swim through their town and walk away on the ice.

While people talked about the tracks, the geese rested well north of the city among bullrushes on the far side of the lake. Here they had neither food nor water, because they could not eat cattail fluff and because the broad rushes were so sinewy tough of fiber even a strong goose would not have been able to break them into small enough pieces for swallowing.

At least they were well hidden. The marsh they were in seemed to stretch endlessly north. Out front the lake was a smooth front of lawn stretching all the way to where the city was barely visible from where they crouched. So Duke did not stand guard, and they both slept warmly all day out of the wind.

Soon as it was dark, Duke moved out of the rushes onto the ice. He continued his trek, but the shoreline turned them west. It wasn't until they came to a wide break in the marsh that Duke could turn north again, and then instinctively he knew he had come back to the river.

They made little progress, because the goose insisted on resting often. Their breastbones were beginning to protrude and part their feathers. What fare they had would not have been enough, even had they been penned and inactive.

The river began to narrow again, but still they did not come to open water. Often Duke angled to the bank to probe, but he found nothing. So that day they made another dry camp, but the pangs of hunger permitted no sleep, so Duke moved out.

The goose looked wearily after him but refused to move. Duke came back, as he had so often, to entice her to try. But she put out her neck and laid it low on the snow after the manner of a goose which has been hurt and is hiding. A dozen times the gander came back, and then in a flurry of rage came up from behind the goose and rapped her sharply with his bill.

She jumped to her feet, haronking as though she'd been hurt, and started north again. Duke went on ahead, and they moved under the starlight, a strange pair for such an alien land, the great proudness of their bearing and the direct purposefulness of their stride gone, so that now they waddled like tame geese, coming down heavily with each step and swaying awkwardly from side to side as though their own weight was too much to bear.

Duke felt the snow getting mushy beneath his webs even

before he suspected they were nearing open water. In the excitement at the feel of it, he left the goose far behind. Then he was floating, and the water was warm around his webs and cool on his tongue and trickling down his long throat. When the goose came up, she was so excited she could not but exclaim, and Duke looked around, alarmed lest her clamoring draw some other danger to them.

After they had sported in the water awhile, Duke swam north and the goose followed. At a shallow rapids they swam into a flock of five goldeneye ducks and sent them skittering in as many directions. They probed the bottom and found a few mollusks and caddis upon which the goldeneyes had been feeding, but they were not strong enough to maintain their positions in the stream, so they swam on to calmer water.

Another small town loomed on the horizon, and when they had swum into it, they found they had another dam to bypass. Duke tried the shore, but all along concrete had been poured to keep the river from running out and coming into the houses which stood along the banks.

Reluctant to go back, Duke toured the banks looking for some way up so they could go on around the dam and be on their way, and that is where daylight caught them, in the middle of the town.

A group of small boys saw them first, and they came to the concrete banks with stones to throw. One hit the goose, and she planed along the water complaining. Duke took to the air, protesting as he lifted. Then he flew above the goose in circles as the boys drove her from one end of the pool to the other. Only the necessity of being at their desks for the opening bell of school sent the boys on their way and saved the goose.

But the word had gotten around that there were two geese below the dam, and people came and, gathering in little groups, took to speculating on why the pair was wintering so far north in Wisconsin, where no goose had wintered before. Some went home to get their cameras and, standing on the dam and the concrete embankments, took pictures.

Duke swam nervously at first in circles around the goose. A man on the dam took bread from a brown paper sack and threw it to the water. Hungry as he was, Duke let it float on past, but the goose swam swiftly to intercept and gobble it.

After school the boys came back to throw stones again, but a man in uniform walked among them and they scattered. Just before dark a woman came to the concrete embankment and carefully poured corn from a coffee can so it fell and bounced around a low rock at the water level.

When it was full dark, except for the lights in town, Duke swam the goose over to where the woman had strewn the corn, and they ate every kernel from off the rock and then began bobbing to collect what they could from the bottom.

It was a fresh grip on life for both of them, and they could feel the strength of the grain coming to their bloodstream as they preened feathers in place. Then, when all but a few of the town's lights had winked out, Duke led the goose far enough south so that they could climb the bank, and together they walked down the main street—two wild geese, in the middle of the road, on past the drugstore, from street light to street light, on past the post office, the grocery store, a hardware store—all the way to the dam, and there they walked out onto the ice above it.

The flowage was a small one. Even in the dark Duke could see its boundaries from where he stood on the ice, and he could see the break in the shoreline trees where the river came in at the far end.

Strengthened now, the goose followed willingly, and soon they came to the river, and it was almost immediately ice free, because here it was not so wide that it spread its strength flatly around. Confined by high banks, it ran swiftly.

But now the current was something to fight. It pushed at them, and their breastbones cleaved it like the bows of small boats, and they left a wake of bubbles as they paddled frantically on their way north. They swam perhaps half a mile an hour—no more—but as daylight was nearing they came to another river which intersected the one they were bucking, and Duke swam excitedly into this new waterway.

There is no way of telling how the gander sensed that this was the river he was looking for. But like a salmon come back to the stream of its birth, the gander, either by taste or smell or some sixth or seventh sense, knew that this waterway was the one. It came out of flatlands, a stream of no great momentum, and on it they made good time, so that when the sun lifted they were nearly a mile up its current.

But it was a barren river, and they found no food. At dawn they rested only a few hours on an ice ledge and then continued swimming. Finally the low banks which held the river disappeared altogether, and on every side there were only flat, frozen marshes. The trickle of open water diminished and then disappeared beneath the ice.

But Duke showed no hesitation now. He pushed himself

up onto the ice and began walking, and he might have gone all the way, except that toward evening the goose played out, and so he sat with her on the ice.

It had thawed during the day, as it sometimes does during a Wisconsin January, and the pair sat in the water on the ice. With the sun gone, the temperature plummeted abruptly. Duke, standing a sleepy guard, was up on one leg, but the goose was down over her webs.

The gander came brightly alert at midnight, and feeling rested, started to move. The goose might have followed, but she was frozen fast. She beat her wings, but the two inches of water into which she had settled had frozen and held her now as firmly as though she'd stepped into a trap.

Duke came back time and again, but the goose could not free herself. Finally he settled down beside her to wait out the night. When morning came he walked off and went so far he was only a speck far up the river.

Frantic, the goose lurched forward, and digging the ice with her wing elbows, she broke free, leaving a mass of feathers behind. She trailed some chunks of ice, but fortunately for her, the thick layer of fluffy down beneath her outer feathers had not been caught up by the ice, so she went with some protection from the cold.

The effort had been so painful she ran for a ways up the river protesting, as though she had pulled free from the jaws of some predator instead of river ice.

Duke heard her, and thinking perhaps some predator had attacked, started back. Then, when he saw her coming, he waited. When she came up alongside, he turned and continued his trek north.

He must have known now that he was near, and he hurried. The goose fell behind, but for Duke there was no waiting. He heard the water before he saw it. He ran and took to the air and flew low until he came to where the creek came down to break open the river. And now, though he had been composed during the long trip, he forgot himself and haronked loudly.

Even the goose, alerted by the gander's excitement, hurried. Then both were in the open river swimming into the creek. Duke went all the way to where widening banks and a natural waterfall made a shallow pool. He hopped over the tiny waterfall and coasted into calm waters. The goose could not maneuver the rushing water, so she laboriously climbed the bank and went around.

Duke knew now they had made it. Not far from the pool he could see the roof of the house and the roof of the hatchery. He haronked once, and from where the geese wintered he heard a chorus of answers. If he wasn't home, this was the closest thing to it.

EPILOGUE

*R*ANK SAW THE GEESE, and when he came with corn Duke did not take to the air but only backed off to the far side of the creek widening. When he had spread the kernels on land and in the water, he walked away, and the goose swam over and began greedily to eat. Duke, though as emaciated as the goose, still stood on ceremony. He waited until she had glutted herself and then swam over to eat with the same restraint a well-fed goose might display.

Rank was visibly impressed and pleased. He stood back far enough so as not to disturb the pair and marveled at what was obviously an earthly miracle. What's more, he took it for an omen, and he couldn't wait to tell Mack, hoping his employer would also take it as a sign and that it would provide the impetus he needed to turn the corner in his life and leave the lonely days behind.

John Mackenna, though he had been escort to various women since his wife had died, had been seeing more and more of a widow, Sarah Greenlee, of late. She was with him when Mack drove into the yard, and Rank, hardly able to keep down the note of triumph in his voice, told them, even before they got out of the car, that Duke was back and he had brought a goose.

Mack took the woman's hand to show her the way, and

in the fading light they stood to watch as the exhausted goose, her crippled wing plain to see, slept floating on the creek widening while the gander, head high, cast a wary eye toward them. In the cold the woman moved closer to the man, but he did not respond by putting an arm around her, since she seemed no pressing thing with him, though a lot of people other than Tom Rank hoped their relationship would become such. And if Mack was impressed, it was not because the gander had brought a goose, but how the pair could possibly have crossed this land in winter and on foot.

"Incredible!" he said as they turned away and started toward the house. "There is no place they could have come from except Heron Marsh. My God, imagine! Across all that ice and snow!"

So the evening was filled with conversation about the geese. Mack told Sarah what he knew about geese in general and specifically about how the gander kept gravitating back to this place where he had lost his mate.

The widow, a striking woman of dark eyes and high color, wisely let him talk, and he wove with a thread of speculation his theory back of the gander's strange behavior, except that in the summing up he had to admit, mostly to himself, that he couldn't fathom the reasons back of it.

Next morning Mack spent several hours watching the pair from a distance with binoculars and then sought out Rank in the hatchery. "They aren't mated," he said.

The foreman put down the hose with which he had been rinsing a vat and, turning, said: "Impossible!"

"It's a fact," Mack said. "He does not treat her like he would if they were mated."

"Then they will be soon enough," the foreman said.

"I suppose so. Soon as the weather breaks," Mack said.

So the two men watched, and there was hardly a day that the goose did not offer herself, but the gander did not take her.

March melted off into April, and water began running in the ditches and the ice turned gray with rot. Songbirds came back, and then one day there was a cut of open water, and a giant, black snapping turtle groped lethargically from the mud toward the light.

Spring kept backing winter north, and in the dark tombs of cocoons were begun quivering resurrections, and a black ant came slowly to a sun-warmed sidewalk.

The quickening was in the soil, pushing forth pale, fragile flowers, and in the tangled brown of winter's dead grasses there was a tint of green. The killdeers came flying in plaintive choirs, grackles arrived in raucous hordes, robins arrived sharp-eyed for the turn of a worm. . . .

Then one day Rank turned the pinioned geese out of their quarters and they went in a wild, winging rush for the ponds clamoring their joy at being free of four walls and winter. The pair at the creek widening heard them, and both stepped to the bank and came to higher ground to where they could see the flock.

The goose started toward the liberated flock, and when the gander failed to follow, she stopped and turned to look at him. He bobbed his head but made no move to follow. She came back. Standing together they watched the geese flail the water in their exuberance. Once again the goose ran toward the pinioned geese. Once again she stopped when the gander failed to follow. Duke took a few steps in her direction and then, dipping his head and talking softly, turned to go back to the creek.

The goose did not follow, but with wings beating the air rushed to join the flock. That afternoon the impatient crippled goose took a mate. Next day, the first northbound flock of geese crossed high above the Silver Sun Ranch. Duke lifted and followed.

Rank and Mackenna watched him go. They stood until he was a speck and then nothing in the sky. Then Tom went back to the hatchery, and John went into the house.

Day after day, both men looked to the sky watching and waiting. Blue herons came. Once an eagle. An osprey pair looked down. Red-tailed hawks hunted the meadow. Black capped night herons were silhouetted against the moon. Egrets stopped briefly. And all manner of wide-winged birds came by, but not Duke.

Summer came, and the crippled goose walked goslings to the water. Fall came, and the leaves fell, and the geese moved across the sky again on their way south, but no gander dropped out of any passing flock to visit.

Then it was winter, and every night when Rank drove home after work there still were no lights in the big, white house except for the little light in the tiny office. And Sarah Greenlee came to the ranch less often and then not at all. And if Duke had died or been killed, then it was his ghost people heard, because on moonlit nights sometimes there a clear, cold fluting from the sky—but perhaps it was only a trick of the wind, because no one ever saw the gander again.